SHE'S UNDER HERE

ALSO BY KAREN PALMER

All Saints

Border Dogs

SHE'S UNDER HERE

a love story,
a horror story,
a reckoning

KAREN PALMER

ALGONQUIN BOOKS
OF CHAPEL HILL
LITTLE, BROWN AND COMPANY

Copyright © 2025 by Karen Palmer

Algonquin Books of Chapel Hill / Little, Brown and Company
Hachette Book Group
1290 Avenue of the Americas, New York, NY 10104
algonquinbooks.com

First Edition: September 2025

Algonquin Books of Chapel Hill is an imprint of Little, Brown and Company, a division of Hachette Book Group, Inc. The Algonquin Books name and logo are trademarks of Hachette Book Group, Inc.

The publisher is not responsible for websites (or their content) that are not owned by the publisher.

The Hachette Speakers Bureau provides a wide range of authors for speaking events. To find out more, go to hachettespeakersbureau.com or email hachettespeakers@hbgusa.com.

Little, Brown and Company books may be purchased in bulk for business, educational, or promotional use. For information, please contact your local bookseller or the Hachette Book Group Special Markets Department at special.markets@hbgusa.com.

Chapter 1, "The Reader Is the Protagonist," was first published in *Virginia Quarterly Review*, vol. 92, no. 2, Spring 2016; and reprinted in *The Best American Essays 2017*, edited by Leslie Jamison (Houghton Mifflin Harcourt; 2017).

Chapter 19 includes J. C. Campbell's checklist, originally published as "The danger assessment: validation of a lethality risk assessment instrument for intimate partner femicide," *Journal of Interpersonal Violence*, 24(4):653–74, in 2004. Retrieved, and used by permission, from www.dangerassessment.org (May 28, 2008).

ISBN 978-1-64375-754-4 (hardcover)
ISBN 978-1-64375-660-8 (ebook)
LCCN 2025936590
Printing 1, 2025
LSC-C

Printed in the United States of America

for
Amy & Erin & Vinnie

[CONTENTS]

"Don't be so fuckin' smart. Things could've gone
the other way, my little nephew."

—Uncle Junior to Tony, *The Sopranos,* "Do Not Resuscitate"

The Reader Is the Protagonist

Once upon a time I disappeared. I was one person one day and the next someone else, both the same woman I'd always been and also utterly, eerily, unfamiliar. There was a story in this, I felt, one built around a universal question: How do you know who you are? Answers would be grounded in the body and bound to memory. But for many years I could not write it. I couldn't figure out where to begin and I had no ending. Moreover, trauma had scrambled my understanding, the need to make meaning stymied by an inability to see. I was unable to sink beneath the surface of events, down to the truth of who had done what and why.

I did talk about the experience, however, details doled out in bits and pieces, if only to certain people under certain circumstances. I usually made of it an adventure; how in 1989, shortly after I married for the second time, my new husband and I buckled my two daughters, then seven and three, into the rear seat of a used car purchased for cash. We'd sold most of our belongings and walked away from the rest, packing up what remained: clothing and toys, pillows and blankets, four place settings, one pot, one pan; and we had a shoebox full of photographs, and my strongbox stuffed with important papers, and cash in a sack, every penny we owned. We told no one where we were going. We meant to vanish. Driving east out of California, we decided on our new names. It might have been exciting, starting over, starting fresh, in a place where we were unknown, but this was do-it-yourself witness protection. Hidden under the driver's seat was a guidebook on how to create new identities, but it couldn't tell us who we'd *be*.

We stopped in Boulder, Colorado. Vinnie—my new husband—had once spent a day in the town, and he remembered it as a friendly place. We drove around for a while. The brick downtown seemed quaint, the neighborhoods leafy and safe. A park with a fast-running creek appealed to the girls. I liked the idea of living near a university, with a tranquil campus, the prospect of lectures and music, young people everywhere.

From a phone booth outside a Safeway, we called a number for a real estate office that we'd found in a local property magazine. Vinnie spoke to the agent on duty and negotiated a trade: a month's rent for painting a condo listed for sale. The arrangement provided immediate relief; we were worried about making our savings last. The agent met us at the property and opened up the garage, empty but for a few rollers and pans and five-gallon buckets of paint. The condo had two bedrooms, two baths, a concrete patio on the other side of sliding-glass doors. The high-ceilinged living room echoed. Such a melancholy sound. The agent handed over the key.

For a week it rained every day. Storms kept us inside, but also, we were shell-shocked, afraid to go out, afraid to be seen. Vinnie and I rolled white paint onto the condo's walls, while the girls colored or watched television on a black-and-white set picked up at Goodwill.

At some point my three-year-old tugged at my legs, her blanket wrapped around her shoulders and a book in her arms: She wanted a story. For more than a year, the demands of everyday life had required all my attention. I'd trusted only what I could touch, what I could see or hear or feel. I had two daughters to protect, and things I'd once seen as essential had fallen away. Books were among the abandoned. One day, halfway through a beloved novel, I set it facedown, and that was the end of that. I couldn't read nonfiction, either, or newspapers, or magazines; that is, nothing meant for adults.

My little daughter leaned against my legs. I set the paint roller in the pan. My older girl joined us, her anticipation charging the air. Reading to my children—this much I could manage.

When I was a child, my mother read to me a lot. Our family life was often fraught, my father uncommunicative, physically absent and emotionally cool, Mom either at his throat or steeped in hostile despair. Reading was her lifelong escape. One effect this had on me was that I believed books were alive, not just the tales within them but the objects themselves. Seated in my mother's lap with a story, the stiffness of the cover told me what it was to have a spine. The words in their regular rows were like heartbeats; the pages, turning, fluttered like wings.

The story my daughters wanted to hear had been their favorite all through the past year: Jon Stone's *The Monster at the End of This Book*.

Grover, one of the characters from *Sesame Street*, is the narrator. Frightened by the monster he imagines awaits him on the last page, he speaks directly to the reader: "Listen, I have an idea. If you do not turn any pages, we will never get to the end of this book."

My daughters looked at me, and I nodded. Together, they turned the page.

Grover ties the next one down with a rope.

Turn.

"You do not know what you are doing to me!" he cries.

Turn.

He nails a page into place. He builds a brick wall.

Turn, turn.

By the end the girls were giggling, breathless from the tension. It didn't matter that they'd heard this story so many times. Fall. Winter. Spring.

"Please do not turn the page," Grover pleads. "Please please please."

Turn.

On the last page Grover exclaims: "Well, look at that! The only one here is . . . ME. I, lovable, furry old Grover, am the Monster at the end of this book."

The reader is the protagonist here. The subject is existential dread. Who is the monster? What does it want, and how will it end? Jon Stone's ingenious construction ensnares the reader. It is also the means of escape. And as is true of every story, the only way out is through.

Vinnie had stopped painting to join us in the condo's living room. The four of us sat cross-legged on the floor, watching rain fall onto the patio. After a while, though, the clouds blew away and we ventured out for a walk to Longs Drugs. The sun dropped into the Rockies, bats flew through the tops of cottonwood trees. The wet grass looked electrified.

The drugstore, hunkered at the corner of Iris and Twenty-eighth, was a beacon, cheerful, full of color and light. You could live out of that store, if you had to; it sold anything you might want in one place. We wandered the aisles. The girls played with makeup samples and inspected a display of discounted summer gear: boogie boards, sand pails and shovels, aluminum beach chairs.

For what beach? I wondered. The ocean was 1,200 miles away.

So was my ex-husband Gil. My daughters' father.

Gil was the reason we'd run—when I left him for an old friend, he'd gone off the rails. He stalked me, and the feeling of being watched and followed, of never knowing where and when he'd appear was a constant torment. He found joy in this and fed off my fear. The prospect of violence excited him. He threatened to shoot Vinnie. He threatened to shoot me. He told me he'd cut off my head and stick it in the refrigerator for the girls to find. And then, months into our separation, he kidnapped our younger child. Nine days he kept her. It felt like nine years. I didn't know where my baby was, or how she was, or even if she was alive.

In 1989 California was still a year away from passing the nation's first anti-stalking law, written after a series of high-profile murders, including those of four women in Orange County who'd been killed by former lovers or former husbands or aspiring suitors.

But when I was divorcing, the authorities could do nothing to help. Even if they had, Gil was unafraid of cops or courts, and I am as certain now as I was then that the threat of jail time would not have deterred him but rather would have inflamed his desire for revenge. I'd gotten my daughter back only by promising to give up someone else I loved, the man for whom I'd left him. That promise was a lie.

At Longs, Vinnie parked himself by the magazines, a newspaper rolled under one arm. He leaned in my direction. We did not touch, but there was heat.

I stared down the rows of paperbacks. Science fiction, horror, westerns, romance. A rack of *New York Times* bestsellers.

Oh, I thought, *books.*

The novel I'd stopped reading months ago—I couldn't recall the plot, or even the title. Once, stories had seen me through everything. They'd been my teachers and companions, my saviors, my family. But standing there, though I felt the shape of their absence, I was unmoved.

BY THE END of our first week in Colorado, I'd secured an interview for a position as a proofreader. The company was an "independent publisher," unnamed in the classified ad. I didn't recognize what a rarity this listing was. The state was just coming out of a recession, and the jobs section of the Boulder paper was thin, with most ads being for food service and minimum-wage retail. In my former life I'd worked as a typesetter, or a secretary, and I felt qualified to proofread, but I worried about being asked for references. On the phone, however, once I said "English major," the interviewer cut things short and requested that I come in.

The publisher's office was in a nondescript two-story building a few blocks north of Boulder's downtown mall. There was no signage out front, only a street number. It was late afternoon and the front door was locked. I rang the bell but no one came. I knocked but there was no answer. I loitered on the sidewalk as rain came down fitfully, moisture disappearing in patches, like footprints erasing themselves.

I rang the bell again. This time a shiny-haired young woman in jeans and a button-down shirt answered. "Hello, Karen," she said decisively. My mind went blank. She was the first person ever to address me by that name.

She led me up a flight of stairs, into a room furnished with a conference table and chairs. We chatted about the weather. "It's late in the summer for the monsoon," she said. I associated monsoons with the tropics, with flooding and disaster; surely that didn't happen here. The young woman said, "But everything changes after

Labor Day." Her manner wasn't unfriendly, exactly, but it wasn't friendly, either.

"What do you publish?" I asked.

She lifted a typescript from a stack on the table and passed it over to me, along with a sharp red pencil. "We can get into that later," she said. "For now, I'd like you to go through this and mark it up for errors. It shouldn't take long."

After she left I skimmed the text, relieved to see nothing technical. But when I returned to the opening sentence, the letters blurred. I couldn't make them cohere. And I panicked, thinking, I really can't read.

Calm yourself—I may have said it aloud. *Look at the spelling.* I ran a hand over the paper; it felt dry, lightly furred. I reread the sentence, concentrating, decided it was fine, and moved on to the next. I saw a mistake and marked the correction. And in this way I worked through the pages. Finished, I set them aside. A preternatural quiet had descended, no sounds of conversation, no hum of office machinery. My mind emptied again, the words from the pages gone. Finally, the young woman returned. She collected the test and whisked it away.

She came back in smiling. She led me along a narrow hallway, into a second, smaller room. Bookcases lined the walls, their shelves packed with softcovers, many workbook-sized and brightly colored, like study guides.

We sat in facing armchairs and chatted, the vibe now affable and benign. Yes, we're new to Boulder, I said. No, I don't ski. Two kids—mostly, I've been home with them.

She looked over my résumé. I expected her to press me about the lack of work history, my inability to provide good references, my nonexistent degree, everything I'd left back in California with my old name. But the young woman shrugged.

"You passed the test. That's all we care about." She herself was a PhD candidate in Classics. "We hire a lot of grad students," she said. "It's a nice group. If you have time today, I'd like you to meet Peder. He's the publisher."

Was it really going to be this easy? I couldn't believe my luck.

She handed me a pamphlet. Its cover read *Paladin Press*.

"Have you heard of us?" she asked.

I had not.

"Okay. So, I'll leave you here on your own for a while. You can browse through the catalogue and have a look at the shelves. You'll get a sense of what we do here." Standing, she said, "If you're okay with it, we'll take the next step."

Alone once more, I opened the pamphlet. I don't know what I expected, some dull corner of academia, or pornography, maybe; it would explain the building's security and air of secrecy. In fact, most of Paladin's books were instructional. Some of the subjects seemed quirky, even fanciful: smuggling, soldiering, locksmithing, espionage. Others were devoted to life off the grid: how to hunt your own food, how to survive in the cold. How to disappear.

That last one forced me from my seat. We'd been in Boulder for a week now, and our guide to creating new identities still sat in the car. Vinnie had purchased it before we left California, from a sur-vivalists' store in LA. But we hadn't read it, at first because we were consumed with fear, and with getting away, and then because we were paralyzed by the enormity of what we'd done. That Paladin had published such a book was only a bizarre coincidence, but it felt like a message to me.

I walked along the shelves, titles jumping out from the books' spines. *Get Even: The Complete Book of Dirty Tricks. 21 Techniques of Silent Killing. Black Medicine, the Dark Art of Death. Deadly Brew: Advanced Improvised Explosives. How to Kill Someone with Your Bare Hands.* My legs shook, a muscle in my cheek throbbed. *Hit Man,* I read: *A Technical Manual for Independent Contractors.* I pulled the volume free.

WHEN WE WERE DATING, Gil used to say to me, "Baby, my life is an open book." He'd offer up candid stories about his difficult childhood in New York, his time in the army, and his various jobs, some of which weren't entirely legal. My father was busy in the world but silent when he came home each night, and I grew up hungry for a man's words. Gil was much older than I was. He spoke warmly and with confidence, and I'd trusted he spoke the truth. He felt like the answer to a question: How do I escape my unhappy home?

Over fourteen years, though, things changed between us. This happened slowly at first, and then all at once. After we married, he bristled at any challenge to his authority. If I complained about his anger or his drinking, his resentments or what I eventually realized were lies, he'd say, "Never judge a book by its cover." This shift in aphorisms was, I think, meant to undermine my reaction to his behavior, and to hint at unacknowledged depths. And then one night he told me, "I once killed a man."

He related the story of the murder at the tail end of a hellishly surreal fight between us that began with a dropped plate but soon enough was about everything. I started the fight, or he did. I don't remember anymore. What I do remember is my desperate need to get away from what he was telling me, running from kitchen to living room to bedroom. We were still living together then, but I'd begun the affair that would end us.

The man he claimed to have killed was someone he'd known back in New York who'd raped a neighborhood girl. The rape was, he said, common knowledge. The man had gotten away with it. This was also common knowledge, a story related in bars.

Gil had been twenty-six at the time, only a few weeks out of the army, unemployed and at loose ends, when he'd run into the alleged rapist at a downtown drinking hole. The man had been in the army, too, some years earlier, and was also unemployed. They had things to talk about, and together shut the place down. Afterward, out on the sidewalk at 2 a.m., Gil suggested a walk. They wound up at the East River. Staring into the water, feeling avuncular, perhaps, the rapist bragged about having "dated" the neighborhood girl. Ugly women, he explained, they need love, too. Gil nodded, steering the man to the river's edge. Then he'd shot him and pushed the body in.

"It was easy," he told me. "Like tossing a piece of trash. No one saw. No one knew. No one ever missed him."

He had me trapped in a corner of the bedroom.

"I don't believe you," I said defiantly.

He pincered my bicep until it burned. *"What you've done to me."*

"You're a monster," I said.

The look on his face was pure astonishment, the change instantaneous, remarkable.

The whole point, he explained, ignoring my terrified moans, was that he'd killed the guy *for* the girl. He was a *hero*. Why couldn't I see it?

"That fuck," he said, "got what he deserved."

In the light of the following day—making the girls their breakfast; overseeing tooth-brushing, and dressing; belongings collected, everybody into the car so I could drive them to school; a numbing drop down into our family routine—Gil's story struck me as impossible in every detail, even laughable. Except for one thing: I knew he sometimes carried a gun. Was the murder true? In the years since, I've never been able to verify it. Maybe it happened by some other means, at some other time. Or maybe the story was invented in every detail. Either way, it meant something to Gil.

A killer, that's how he saw himself. It's how he wanted me to see him, as someone to be mortally feared. He was teaching me, in the clearest possible way, what he was capable of.

In that book-lined room at Paladin Press, I clutched *Hit Man* to my chest.

Well, I held some book close. It's possible it was another title. I don't think it matters. My apprehension of the work Paladin was sending into the world, the ugliness of it, and how close to home, made me drop the book to the floor: The pages might have burst into flames. I ran out of the room, a matter of self-preservation, and rushed along the deserted hallway, down the stairs, out the front door, and onto the street.

MY DAUGHTERS' DELIGHT in *The Monster at the End of This Book* lasted for years, long past when it should have grown stale. There is such pleasure in fear, the thrill of being alive. In Jon Stone's story, the reader becomes the means by which poor Grover moves ever nearer his fate, the monster at the end of the book. Repeating the journey makes for a different kind of pleasure, the ending always the same and therefore harmlessly known.

After my interview at Paladin Press, I picked up a pizza and returned to the condo.

"How'd it go?" Vinnie asked.

"I didn't get it," I said.

He took the white box from me and set it on the kitchen counter and folded me up in his arms. The girls, drawn by the sound of my voice, buzzed around us. In that moment I felt so safe. My loved ones were right there. Later, after the girls went to bed, Vinnie and I would talk about Paladin. I'd tell him how suited I might have been for a job I could never do, because of a room where instruction on how to perpetrate violence kept company with guides on how to escape.

But now it was time to eat.

I cut up the pizza, Vinnie and I got out the dinner plates, the four of us sat on the living-room floor. Through the sliding glass doors we watched rain fall onto the concrete patio. When the clouds blew away, we walked the by-now-familiar blocks to Longs. In the periodicals aisle, Vinnie flipped through a magazine. The girls were curled up at his feet, absorbed in comics. He smiled at me over their heads.

Ten days earlier, we'd married at the top of a hill on Santa Catalina Island; our witness was a city gardener. We'd had only the one afternoon, and I'd been seasick on the ferry over, and standing under a tree, reciting my vows, I'd felt dizzy and hungry and deeply in love. All around us, leaves had shimmered vertiginously.

I stared down that same display of paperback books. Science fiction, horror, westerns, romance. A countdown of *New York Times* bestsellers. They wanted only for someone to open them, that the stories might live.

We disappeared, I thought. And I felt hollowed out, as if I might fill that empty space with anything.

I don't know what I pulled from the rack. Maybe *Cat's Eye*—I remember reading the novel that year. Or maybe it was *Love in the Time of Cholera*, or *Riding the Iron Rooster*. Maybe it was one of those six-hundred-page family sagas I'd devoured as a teen, the cover fussy with cutouts and gold-embossed lettering.

I opened the book and started to read.

It was, I knew, a beginning.

When it was full dark, it was time to leave. We stood in line at the register, paid cash for ice-cream bars and an *Atlantic Monthly* and my paperback. Out on the street we all held hands. At the corner we stopped for a light. Cars came and went all around us, headlights and taillights shining white, shining red. We were out in the open, fully exposed, and I shivered though it was summertime still. I dug in the bag for my paperback, wedged it under one arm. The light changed and we crossed.

2

She's Under Here

It was not the first time I ran.

Picture this: me, standing at the corner of Griffith Park Boulevard and St. George, tucked up against the nine-foot-high retaining wall of John Marshall High School's athletic field. A brisk spring day in Los Angeles, wind tossing the tops of palm trees. Arms crossed against the chill, I had one knee bent, the wooden sole of my Baretraps sandal set flat against the wall in an attempt to look alluringly casual. On the sidewalk beside me sat a small round suitcase. Inside it I'd packed a silky blue halter dress, a toothbrush, and a clean pair of cotton bikini underpants.

I glanced at my watch. Quarter past noon. Gil was late.

When the lunch bell rang, students swarmed from every building. Some gathered in cliques on the quad, others continued onto the field. Still others left campus to eat out or toke up. Most would return after lunch, though the chronic ditchers were done for the day. The odd senior might have enough credits to legitimately take off early. As a recent transfer from an all-girls Catholic high, I was one of these; by this time I was usually on a bus and halfway to my job. But not today. This was just fine, because Gil was my boss. He owned an office-supply company staffed with actors who sold copy paper over the phone. I was the seventeen-year-old part-time secretary. Gil was thirty-six, a father of three, divorcing but not yet divorced.

A station wagon with fake wood paneling rolled to a stop. I ignored it—Gil drove a taxicab-yellow VW bug. The driver hit the horn. I bent to look, and there was Gil. His head bobbed, the heels of his hands beat the steering wheel. The lock on the passenger door popped and the window lowered. Blast of electric guitar. Gil angled himself across the bench seat. He called my name— "Kerry!"—and it was like I'd never heard it before. He gave me his evil curly-lipped grin. I thought he was a dead ringer for Jack Nicholson in *Easy Rider*, well, except for the beige slacks and black zip-up Florsheim boots.

"Want a ride, little girl?"

I stepped to the curb. "Where'd you get this?" I asked, meaning the station wagon.

"It's Rita's," he said.

Rita was Gil's soon-to-be-ex wife. She lived in a house in Studio City with their young children, while he rented a ratty studio apartment a few blocks from the office.

"Why do you have Rita's car?"

Gil waggled a Nicholson brow. "It's a long drive to Vegas, baby."

I reached for the handle. The lock thunked shut. "Say please," Gil teased. "Pretty please."

I was already going back for my bag.

Wild howls sounded from the field atop the retaining wall— *Fuck you! Get the fuck off!*—followed by girly screaming. Up there, where I couldn't see them, were chicks I didn't know and boys I didn't want to. My stomach lurched, and for a moment I felt so alone. I lifted my suitcase. It weighed almost nothing.

Gil watched me walk back to him. "Jesus, your *legs*."

I had on a short gray skirt, black tights, and a houndstooth vest from a little boy's suit layered over a long-sleeved black leotard. I'd bought this costume at a thrift store, thinking it was arty—I fancied myself that kind of girl.

"You look like a fawn," Gil said, pushing open the passenger door.

Heat climbed my chest, my neck, my face. It wasn't that I'd never heard such things before (*Hey fox, let's get that bra off*), but I was pretty sure no one else ever meant it.

I'd known Gil for exactly three weeks.

A phone room, I'd discovered, was a fun place to work. Gil took care of his fledgling salesmen, and they adored him. Why wouldn't they? He roamed from cubicle to cubicle giving pep talks, listening to pitches, dispensing pointers and fatherly advice. He paid better than most and always bought lunch, and he accommodated their crazy audition schedules. A few he'd even bailed out of life-derailing jams. At my desk typing up invoices, I heard it all.

And when the workday was done and everyone else had gone home, he and I would sit at a conference table and talk.

Or, rather, Gil talked. I didn't mind.

My parents were transplanted New Yorkers, and Gil's accent sounded like theirs. His sense of humor—quick and dry, with a hint of sadism—was also familiar, except that, unlike my parents, Gil brought me in on the joke, even when I didn't get it, maybe especially when I didn't get it, and if I recognized cruelty I ignored it, because he made me feel safe. I'd study his thick-lashed hazel eyes and wavy collar-length hair, only half paying attention while he bragged about the business. The nitty-gritty of office-supply sales bored me, but I admired his ambition, his bald glee at having money in his pocket. I loved how an old woman in a coffee shop had once told him he had the looks and bearing of Buffalo Bill, whom she'd met in a Wild West show when she was a child.

His stories about having grown up poor in Manhattan mesmerized me: seven people crammed into a railroad flat in Yorkville, with a john in a closet and a hulking bathtub two steps from the stove. The tub's plywood cover doubled as a kitchen counter; if you wanted to bathe, you had to take everything off it, and everyone had to get out of the room. Gil and his brothers slept on itchy horsehair mattresses in the front parlor, Gil eyeballing the action on York Avenue from their third-story window. Everyone listened to the family's Philco radio: Jack Benny, *Fibber McGee & Molly*, *Amos 'n' Andy*. When Gil was older, he'd take his little sister to an ice cream parlor up on Eighty-sixth Street, and they'd order Chocolate Pecan Tulip Sundaes and eat them in a sugar frenzy, laughing so hard—he couldn't remember why—she always got sick.

His mother still lived in that rent-controlled apartment. She kept everything immaculate; Gil wanted me to know how much he valued that. Mutti spoke little English but had worked for forty years as a housemaid on Park Avenue. His father, a former German merchant marine who'd jumped ship in New York Harbor, had died of a heart attack at age eighty-two, roofing a brownstone in Boerum Hill. I don't miss him, Gil said, not one bit. Vati had been a drunk and a bully. He'd beaten Mutti, chasing his boys around the apartment when they defended their mother. Gil hated him, while acknowledging he'd turned out more like the old man than any of his siblings.

Leaning back in his fancy boss's chair, he confessed to shoplifting as a kid, to rolling drunks for pocket change and peeping on neighbors. At seventeen, while visiting an aunt in Connecticut, the cops arrested him for breaking and entering several houses in town. He spent six months in the Danbury jail. Gil made a sweeping gesture, dismissal or absolution of his wayward young self, and waited to see if I'd bite. I was a quiet, bookish girl, so obviously middle-class, with my glasses and temperamental skin and love of playing the piano, that I might have been mistaken for someone easily shocked; but the truth was I'd never gone for the cute boys or the mommy-pleasers, the A students or the jocks. I'd been drawn only to bad boys, slinky-hipped delinquents who could teach me something.

Our conference-room conversations ran long, and then longer, and I was often late getting over to California Hospital to relieve my mother, who stayed with my father all day every day, reading and praying and harassing the nurses. I spent evenings with Daddy, who was recovering from the surgical removal of his cancerous voice box. No longer able to speak, he communicated by scribbling on notepads, fuming when no one could read his handwriting. Once a newspaperman, later press secretary to the mayor of Los Angeles, he was currently on medical leave from his job as a City Council deputy. In the first month of his illness, a parade of visitors had passed through his room; the man could talk to anyone, it seemed, except me. I thought it was his fault, he thought it was mine. I'd help him with dinner, then slouch in the vinyl chair next to his hospital bed, eyes down, concentrating on schoolwork while he watched TV. I laid low in plain sight, while also wanting credit for being a dutiful daughter. Every now and then, Daddy would point at the water pitcher, or his pillows, or he'd write something down. *Can you look for the lotion?* The later it got, the more my presence seemed to annoy him, but when I stood to leave, his face paled and his eyes went wild. I resented this and couldn't wait to escape. Being around my parents, especially Daddy, was unbearable. I didn't understand that he was scared to be alone.

Tonight, I'd told Mom I was skipping the hospital to sleep over at my girlfriend Pam's. Pam was the one person I still talked to from my old Catholic high school. Mom trusted her. More crucially, these days she trusted me; pregnancy, the worst thing that could happen to any girl, had already happened to me. I'd been taught since childhood that having sex was playing with fire, but I'd failed to fully imagine the consequences. And I'd survived a home for unwed mothers, but not without scars. It was why I'd had to change schools, why I felt alienated from other teens. Giving away my baby had crushed my heart. It also made me reckless. And that left me open to someone older, someone experienced, someone exciting.

Gil patted the station wagon's seat. "C'mon, get in."

We'd not yet had sex. We'd barely kissed. An overnight escape to Las Vegas would be our first date. "This," he announced, "is going to be great."

A lick of heat in my belly. I tossed my suitcase into the back, slid in, and pulled shut the heavy door.

This.

GIL SAID THAT the Stardust was his favorite hotel. Whenever he came to Vegas, this was where he stayed. He loved the casino's sparkly façade, the spacious rooms, the swimming pools, the inexpensive buffet. He'd always had good luck at the tables.

The line at check-in stretched around the lobby. We advanced holding hands, but when we were nearly at the counter, Gil told me to go wait by the elevators. In the office the age difference between us dissolved, but renting a room, even in Las Vegas, might get touchy. I was underage and looked it, five foot three and one hundred pounds. I might have been his daughter.

After a quick exchange with the clerk, Gil strode over to me. "There's a convention in town," he announced. "No room at the inn." He took my elbow and steered me toward the casino entrance.

But what about . . . *privacy?* I'd assumed that sex was why we were here.

"No one sleeps in Vegas," he scoffed.

I told him I needed to change.

"You can use the ladies'."

In the restroom toilets flushed and taps ran. Women gathered at the sinks, fussing with clothing and combing their hair. They leaned toward mirrors, voices tight, mouths tensed as they reapplied their lipstick. I shut myself up in a stall, bent to unbuckle my Baretraps, kicked them free, and peeled down my tights. Off came the skirt, then the leotard. I stood barefoot on the tile wearing only panties.

My breasts were fuller than before the baby, the areolas still dark, and a pale brown line ran up my skin from pubis to ribcage. There was a subtle slackening to my belly. Objectively, I supposed, my body was nice enough, as long as you didn't know what to look for, but I was self-conscious. When I was fifteen, I'd let a high-school senior, an antisocial friend of a friend, take *Penthouse*-style photos of me. Up in the boy's attic bedroom, drunk on his dad's hundred-proof Maker's Mark, I'd climbed gamely onto a waterbed and sloshed around with peacock feathers and scarves and dangly Bob Guccione pearls, dizzied by the flashing camera and the knots in the pine walls that spun like cartoon galaxies. Already, at seventeen, I wished I had those photographs, proof I'd once looked like other girls.

I unzipped my suitcase, pulled out the blue halter dress, and shoved my school clothes inside. Silk dropped over my head; it skimmed my torso and hips. I tied the dress at the neck, stepped out of my panties, and stuffed them in the bag. I left the bag in the stall. When I emerged from the ladies', my cheeks were burning, whether from pleasure or embarrassment I couldn't have said.

Gil was waiting, smoking a cigarette, a shoulder pressed to a wall.

He looked me up and down and whistled. Two cocktail waitresses carrying trays of drinks passed between us. "I'm gonna teach you blackjack, baby," he said. "It's the only game where the player's odds are as good as the house." And one of the waitresses laughed.

WE MADE A beeline for the tables, Gil choosing one according to a mysterious formula he did not explain. He climbed onto an end stool and took out five one-hundred-dollar bills. A pretty blonde dealer used a plastic grip to push his money through a slot in the felt, then slid a stack of chips over to Gil. A cocktail waitress magically appeared at his side. "JB rocks," he said. "Bring two. And keep 'em comin', honey."

Chips and cards. Expansion, contraction. The mirrored ceiling darkly reflected arms as they reached across the table, the players' exposed wrists, and the vulnerable tops of heads. There are watchers up there, Gil said, an eye-in-the-sky that looked for card-counters and crooked dealer-player alliances.

I observed several rounds, hoping to absorb the rules. But then I grew restless, so I wandered away. I passed a lounge where a flame-haired pianist played Debussy's "Clair de lune," a piece I'd performed in my first real recital; the music reminded me of home, of hours spent practicing, Mom in the next room calling out clunkers. I passed the *Lido de Paris* showroom, rows of crap tables and clacking roulette wheels. I stopped to watch a high-stakes poker game, stone-faced players seated at a table in a room behind glass—the men in tuxedos, the women in cocktail dresses, bloodred and wedding-gown white—then drifted through a field of slot machines, all sirens and bells, coruscating light and change rattling in cardboard buckets, the air a miasma of cigarette smoke, body odor, and battling perfumes. And I remembered being in Reno with my parents when I was twelve, stuck at the lip of Harrah's lobby, too young to get in. I'd sat on the floor and watched Mom pulling the mechanical arm, drinking her drink and smoking her smoke, the look on her face the same whether she won or lost.

I had an urge now to play but no cash. My wallet was stashed in my suitcase, abandoned in a ladies' room stall. My driver's license and twenty dollars were surely gone. I didn't care. Because *this* was the world. Nothing existed beyond these walls; there was no Los Angeles, no John Marshall High; I had no mother, no father, no home. I could be anyone.

I could be someone who was with Gil.

I found him at the blackjack table as I'd left him. Without looking up he said, "Thought maybe you ran into a high roller and scrammed."

In my absence his chips had multiplied. "How much is that?" I asked. The dealer dealt herself an ace; she'd made 21. She swept the losers' chips away.

"A thousand or so." Gil sighed. "But you should've seen me an hour ago. I was up more . . . Listen, why don't we visit the shops. I'll buy you something to put 'round that pretty neck. I should feed you, too. You hungry? Surf and turf, how's that sound? Or we could see a show. . . ."

I leaned into him, pressed my breasts into his back. He slipped from the stool. "Hop on up, baby, and give it a whirl."

"I don't have any money. I lost my bag."

"How'd you manage that?" A huge grin. "Never mind, I'll spot you."

Well, and why not?

He placed the first bet for me, pushing the chips forward, fifty dollars' worth. To earn that much I had to work for a week.

The dealer dealt. I took up my cards. I glanced at Gil, seeking direction, but he shook his head. So I played the hand on my own. And I was lucky, I won. I won the next hand, too, and the next. It felt like soap bubbles rising, rainbows caught in each one. I split a pair of kings and doubled down, as I'd seen Gil do. He lifted the hair from the back of my neck and kissed my nape, little jolts of electricity. "I'm your good luck," he murmured. "And you're mine."

I glanced up at the eye in the sky. Were the watchers watching us? Suddenly, I wanted to quit while I was ahead, to keep what I'd already won.

AT THE ENTRANCE to the *Lido*, Gil passed a folded bill to the usher. The tip disappeared into a pocket, then the usher escorted us down descending terraces of round tables to a prime spot left of center stage. "Thanks, this is great," Gil said. To me he said, "Isn't this great?"

He flagged a waitress and ordered cocktails, two JB rocks for himself, two Harvey Wallbangers for me.

"What's a Harvey Wallbanger?" I asked.

"Orange juice," the waitress said. "Vodka. Galiano."

"You'll like it, baby, it's sweet." When the waitress turned away, Gil grabbed her arm. With his other hand he made a victory sign. "Two more each." To me he said, "You can never get their attention during the show." Soon, eight tumblers covered our table. It seemed a frightening amount of alcohol.

All my life I'd been around booze. My mother loved her martinis, as did many of her generation, but Daddy was a binge drinker. For weeks he'd nurse glasses of iced ginger ale, until one night he'd go to a bar and order a beer, or someone would order it for him and he wouldn't refuse. He'd come home with a six-pack of Coors. One six-pack became two, beer became whiskey, then he'd crash in the bedroom while Mom moved into the den. The next day she'd call him in sick to City Hall before she went off to work. Mom cleaned and cooked dinner; she asked about school and inspected homework. Late at night, though, she cried on the couch; my room shared a wall with the den and I heard. Sometimes I went to her. She'd be saying a rosary in the dark, her own drink close to hand. If I tried to climb in, she'd tense, as if there was no room. "Things'll look different tomorrow, Kerry," she'd say, "just go back to bed." And in the morning, I'd find the notes she left around the house for Daddy. On the toilet, *Clean up your piss!*, on the fridge, *Eat something, Ray!*, on their closed bedroom door, *Do you want me to bring your daughter in here? Do you want her to see?* When she couldn't contain her disgust, she'd burst in, pleading and screaming. Sometimes, she dragged me with her, a cruel testament to her desperation. She'd stand me by the side of the bed and fling back the covers, exposing Daddy on the soiled sheet curled up like a snail. I shut my eyes but I saw. Worse was the sound of flesh on flesh, Mom hitting Daddy in the back and shoulders until, rising from his stupor, he shot out an arm and struck her in return. I cried, but they didn't hear. I wanted to get between them, but I was a child and I froze. Five years old. Ten years old. Thirteen. How many times? I don't know. In the end, their shame became mine. I wanted to disappear.

All we could do was wait. After a week or two, something would switch off inside Daddy and the binge ended. He'd rise early, shower and shave, put on a suit, a starched shirt and silk tie, the wingtips he paid me a dime to polish. He'd walk me down the hill to school, holding my hand and promising *never again*. It was a promise he couldn't keep.

Gil peered at me over the top of his glass. All around us the showroom chattered and throbbed. I took a wary sip of my Wallbanger. It was indeed sweet. Gil nodded encouragement. The whites of his eyes were threaded with veins. He was drunk. I'd sworn I'd never date a drinker, but at the same time I wanted Gil, so I convinced myself he was nothing like my father. Gil was a lover of life. He'd never hide away with a bottle. He'd never ruin his family. See? Here he was toasting his excellent fortune, and mine; laughing and talking; talking to me.

We were in Vegas and this was how it was done.

I finished one cocktail, then another. I hadn't eaten in hours and was instantly wrecked.

The lights went down all at once. The room quieted. The orchestra played, showgirls floating out from the wings in a swoon of violins. Some wore full costumes while others were topless, dressed in sequined bikini bottoms and headdresses half again as tall as they were, and in their high heels they were all impossibly long-limbed, with breasts impossibly round, dancing Amazons with wide white smiles and masklike makeup. The stage rose, revealing a small ice-skating rink. A female performer who looked like a professional did figure eights. Surreptitiously, I watched Gil. His eyes glistened. He was a man, and men liked looking at naked girls. I liked looking at them, too. The music changed. The dancers changed costumes and attitudes, like mechanical dolls. And I remembered an old Mills Brothers song Daddy sang to me when I was small: "I'd rather have a paper doll to call my own, than have a fickle-minded real live girl." I'd loved my father then, that mysterious man who smelled of aftershave, who pitched plastic golf balls at a hated oil painting above our fireplace, and called my mother not Dorothy but Dar-a-thee. "Once in love with Amy, always in love with Amy." My parents had a 45 record of Ray Bolger singing that song. He was the Scarecrow in *The Wizard of Oz*, and, magically, he shared Daddy's first name. But, as with *Paper Doll*, the lyrics made me sob with jealousy. And Daddy would laugh, and Mom would scold, *Don't tease her, Ray.*

Up on the stage, two men gestured and paced. They locked a woman in a wooden box and sawed her in half. They stuffed her into a wardrobe and *poof!*, she vanished. There was more, but I couldn't follow it. And all at once there was an explosion of white, doves flying, aimed at a lighted window cut into the top of the showroom's back wall.

It was over. The audience applauded. The lights came up. Gil and I joined the exiting crowd.

Out in the casino the throng dispersed. My stomach lolloped from all the alcohol. My neck ached from the air-conditioning.

I thought of my father in his hospital bed, his room so cold it cut off blood to the tip of his nose. I thought of the stainless-steel tube that held open the hole in his neck where his larynx used to be. Whenever the tube clogged with phlegm, he'd press the call button for a nurse to come and clear it, but if he couldn't wait, he'd yank the tube free and hold it out to me. Standing at the little sink in his room, I'd run the tap, fighting nausea, my hands shaking when they needed to be steady and quick, because without that tube, he'd suffocate.

And Mom? She was awake this very second, I was sure of it,

her mind arcing toward me across miles. She loved me better than anyone, and read me better, too, no matter how I might hide. She'd know I'd lied about going to Pam's. There was nothing my mother hated more than a liar.

I thought of the magicians' doves. Their white underbellies, their white wings, their pursuit of the light.

"I have to go home," I told Gil. "You have to take me home."

WE STOOD AT the western edge of the Stardust's enormous parking lot, me by the passenger door of the station wagon, yanking stupidly on the locked handle, Gil slouched against the rear bumper. He was refusing to drive me back to LA, refusing even to look for a motel. He wanted to sleep in the car.

I stared at the back of his skull rising boxlike above the wagon's roof. During one of our conference room talks, he'd told me his father used to call him Blokkopf—Blockhead.

Perfect, I thought.

Then I pictured the boy he used to be. The flat-headed middle child of five, the troublemaker, neglected, never the favorite. Contrite, I sidled around and planted myself in front of him. I gazed up into his eyes. They were half-shut, red-rimmed. Whiskers stippled his chin, a few grays shining like bits of tinsel.

"I can drive," I said.

Gil fished in a pocket. He pulled out his car keys and dangled them, an offering, but when I reached he snatched them away. He shoved me, hand flat on my chest. It was not a hard shove but casual, as if knocking aside a thing of no consequence. I staggered back, too stunned to be mad.

Our end was in this beginning, but I didn't see.

Maybe because Gil pulled me toward him and kissed me. He tasted of whiskey, of cigarettes and cinnamon gum. He tasted of the unknown.

My parents—what could they do to me, after all? Nothing.

I should've been afraid. Instead I felt free.

I climbed into the rear of the station wagon and stretched out on a black rubber mat. Gil lay beside me. He wriggled to shed his sweater, folded it, and placed it under my swimming head. "Mom never lets me have pillows," I said. "She thinks it'll keep my backbone straight. When I was a kid, I wasn't even allowed to sleep with stuffed animals—she tucked me in with Jesus and Mary statues, one on either side of my head."

"What do you mean, statues?"

"Oh, you know. Something to pray to. Mary was made of wood, Jesus was painted plaster. They were hard as rocks."

"You're kidding," Gil said.

"No, my mom's really religious. She wanted the statues to stand guard, to whisper truth into my sleeping ears. She'd sing me a hymn, 'Holy God, We Praise Thy Name.' There's a line, 'All in heaven above adore Thee.' When I was little, I thought it was 'All in heaven above *a Dorothy*.' That's Mom's name. I figured everyone up there knew her."

Gil said dreamily, "Tell me about your bedroom."

My walls were painted yellow, a double bed tucked tightly into an alcove. I had a pistachio-green desk and two small white dressers, and in one corner a skinny built-in closet. The closet's warped wooden door wouldn't shut all the way, and I used to watch the gap for shadows smoking out into the room. That's the devil, Mom told me. When I said I didn't believe in the devil, she said, That's funny, because he believes in you.

But I didn't tell Gil all that.

"What's in your closet?" he asked.

"Dresses. Skirts and shirts. School uniforms."

"Plaid?"

"No. A pleated navy-blue shift."

"What else?"

"There's a pile of shoes on the floor."

"What else?"

How did he know?

On the shelf at the top of the closet, hidden behind a stack of board games, was my most valued possession, a small fireproof strongbox from Sears. I'd bought it at Mom's suggestion. Some things, she said, can never be replaced. She and Daddy had one just like it in the den, stuffed with mortgage papers, birth certificates, Daddy's honorable discharge from the Army Air Corp, the adoption agreement with Holy Family Services that made them my parents and me their child.

"You didn't tell me you were adopted," Gil said. "How long have you known?"

"I can't remember ever not knowing."

"What about your real parents?"

"Mom and Daddy are my real parents."

"Hmm," he said. Then, "What's in the strongbox?"

Two things only: a love note from a teenage boy I'd met when I'd hitchhiked home from a summer day at the beach, and a Polaroid photograph of our son. The teenager I seldom thought of anymore, though briefly I'd loved him, his physical grace, his inarticulate charm, the way he'd tossed his sideswept hair from his eyes. But my baby. The photo had been taken by temporary foster parents, an older couple who'd cared for my son before he went to live with his new family. They'd posed him propped up against a sofa cushion, his small body lost in a baggy yellow sleeper. I looked at the Polaroid only when certain of being alone. Hands shaking, I'd trace my finger along my son's cheek. My parents thought I'd gotten over giving him up, but I hadn't, and never would.

Gil went up on one elbow. He studied me so intently my toes curled.

I told him about my son.

"Oh *wow*," he said. "How'd you *do* it?"

I stiffened at the criticism. "I wasn't given a choice."

"That's not right. You always have a choice."

I went perfectly still, hot all the way to my core. The day I met Gil I'd changed the combination on the strongbox's lock to 6-5-3, his height and mine. That's how sure I'd been about him. But now I saw he belonged nowhere near my son.

He buried his fingers in my hair and tugged. "You did what had to be done. That takes balls."

My eyes filled with tears. I'd misread him. He wasn't criticizing. On the contrary, he understood.

"It's like me with the wagon," he said.

He told a long story then about how, at dawn, he'd driven the yellow VW bug over to Studio City. He'd parked a block from the house where he used to live and walked. The lights were out, the locks changed months ago, but he still had his clicker and used it to get into the garage. The rising door clanked and groaned. Gil was certain Rita would hear, and the kids, certain everyone would come running. No telling what Rita might do. She could be violent. He pointed to a scar in his left eyebrow as proof.

"I had to do it," he said.

There was something wrong with this story, and something

wrong with being here in Gil's car, which was his wife's. But it had been a long day and his hand in my hair felt so good.

He whispered into my ear, "I'd do anything for my kids."

The words filled me with longing.

Soon it would be tomorrow. We'd go back to the casino and cash in our chips. All that money, coins dropped into a pool. I was dropping, too . . . down, and down . . . and then I was up on hands and knees, hair tumbled into my face. My throat ached, and a hard hot pressure pulsed behind my eyes. I clawed at the rubber mat.

The inside of the car shined. My body was filling with light.

"Kerry!" Gil shook my arm. "Wake up! You're having a nightmare." He rubbed the groove between my shoulder blades and smoothed a hand down my spine. I collapsed with a groan.

The light—it wasn't mine. The sun was up, it was morning, that was all.

Gil's palm rested on my hip. His fingers kneaded my flesh through the silk, and I thought of a cat exercising its claws. Desire flooded through me, followed by dread. I was in Las Vegas, in the back of a station wagon with a man twice my age, a man who said he'd do anything for his kids.

Gil cupped my ass. His fingertips trilled the inside of my thigh. I wanted him to stop but I also wanted more. He rolled his torso over mine, his breath warming the back of my neck. "You were jabbering, baby," he said. "Digging like a dog for a bone, saying over and over, 'She's under here.'"

3

Ordinary Life

In our first apartment, on Wilton Place in LA, our second-story bedroom windows faced bedroom windows in the building next door, and sometimes late at night Gil and I were awakened by the sounds of lovemaking. Other times, we heard a couple fighting. We saw them occasionally, too, if their lights were on and ours off. The man's dark hair was brush cut, while she had a platinum forelock, like a palomino pony; she was stocky and tanned, he pigeon-chested and pale.

One hot summer night, I surfaced to the sound of high heels clacking up the walkway. Jangle of keys and female muttering. Across the way a lamp snapped on. The young man came to his open window and stuck his head out. "Fuckin' bitch! I changed the locks!" As the young woman's weeping burbled up like water, he called down, "You're lucky you can't get in!"

The light snapped off. The heels clacked away. Gil threw an arm over me, and I snaked a leg around him. We were luxuriating in the superiority of our love.

And when I was almost asleep, drifting in that liminal space of waking dreams, Gil murmured, "She got what she deserved."

IT WAS THE late 1970s, the last gasp of the pre-AIDS era. The world was awash in casual sex. Everyone drank, everyone smoked, everyone was funny and fast. Discos were cool. Drugs were cool. Enough was never enough. Gil's friends, who were now my friends, called him Mr. Fun. There was Mike, who'd worked with Gil at Xerox; Gun Dog, whose print shop doubled as a hangout; Charlie, a kid from Boston's North End stuck on the West Coast because he was in trouble back home; Buster, a homicide cop out of notorious Rampart Station; and Alan, who bartended at the Bounty in the Gaylord Hotel. I was the only woman, the so-called *best girl in LA*. I liked that, exemplifying a term I wouldn't know for decades: internalized misogyny. The important thing was that Gil was proud of me. I basked in the warmth of his approval. Because he was beloved. I saw it in how the guys looked at him, how they hung on his every word. He was our common denominator, our master of ceremonies. A raconteur and a mimic, he'd do anything to make the guys laugh: jump off a rooftop into a pool, shimmy up a flagpole, eat flowers out of a vase at a fancy restaurant. He paid for everyone's liquor. He shared his cocaine. He loaned out money and fronted anyone brave enough to start a business. Gil used shadiness as social cachet, dealing weed out of Gun Dog's print shop. At parties he showed off his multiple driver's licenses in multiple names. He boasted about not filing taxes. Most of the business's profits, I'd learned, came from selling stolen supplies. A former partner had cleaned Gil out years ago, but instead of going to the police, he was still taking it out in trade. Gil brought a gun to these meetings. The former partner did the same. To me the gun was an abstraction, an item stashed in a file cabinet at the office. The whole situation seemed improbable, and hilarious. Why were salesmen playing with guns?

ON THE TENTH floor of a seedy downtown high-rise, Gil sat at a kitchen table with a dome-headed old man. There were only two chairs, so I stood behind Gil. The old man rummaged in a pants pocket, pulled out a royal-blue velvet box, and opened it up, revealing a diamond ring.

"It was my wife's," he said. "One-and-a-half carats."

When Gil held the ring to the light, the old man said, "There's a flaw, but no one will see."

Gil reached back and captured my wrist. He looked at me upside-down and blinked, his eyelids seemingly rising to close, which made him look alien. His mouth moved. I didn't know what he was saying, and then I did. *Marry me.*

A FEW WEEKS BEFORE the wedding, I caught Gil with another woman in the night-soaked alley behind the Executive Room, a dive bar made famous by Billy Joel's "Piano Man." The woman looked like Tammy Wynette, all poufy blonde hair and calico. Stricken, I watched them fucking. Why couldn't Gil see me, I wondered, or sense me?

Later, when I asked if he loved her, he said, "This is what a man does. But I love only you."

And instead of breaking us up, it made me want him more.

SOMETIMES I THINK I married him just to prove that I could.

THE GIRL IN THE MIRROR was pretty in the way of all young brides, her expression innocently knowing. Her lips were darkened, her cheekbones highlighted, her eyes shined. Daisies and roses were pinned into her curls. Her legs were encased in silky stockings, feet like candies in their strappy satin high heels. The dress was one-of-a-kind, the material off-white tea-length organza with thin satin ribbons that circled the hem. It had short sleeves, a fitted bodice, a simple scooped neck. In the back pearl buttons ran from waist to nape. The bride had sewed this confection herself. Now, with the ceremony only an hour away, it still wasn't finished. Three times I'd laid out the bodice; three times I'd set in the sleeves; three times the buttonholer had shredded the delicate fabric. Out of organza, I superglued a half-inch strip of selvage over the ruined edge. I would have to be stitched into this dress, and torn free.

ONE MINUTE I was standing at the rear of the church, waiting to enter; the next, Gil and I ran arm-in-arm down the aisle. The wedding party assembled outside for pictures, blinking in the sun like blind mice. Mom slipped on her sunglasses. Behind them she was crying, but I wouldn't know that for months, when the packet of photos arrived in the mail.

WE'D BEEN MARRIED for less than six months when two uniformed officers knocked on the door. I was alone in the apartment—they were seeking Gilbert W_____. "Does he live here?" they asked. I shook my head, denial instinctual. They showed me a copy of Gil's driver's license and pointed to his photo. "Recognize him?" Again I shook my head. The officers thanked me and left. I locked the door and leaned against it, eyeing the cartons of stolen toner that climbed our staircase. Minutes later Gil strolled in with deli sandwiches. "Pastrami, Kerry! Your favorite!" I told him he'd just missed the police. I told him I didn't give them a thing. "That's my girl!" Gil cried, and I flushed. Did this make me a . . . *moll?*

MITHRIDATISM: PROTECTING ONESELF against poison by gradually self-administering nonlethal amounts.

AND THEN: *oh, this baby.* Seven long years I'd waited for her. She was born with dark hair, dark eyes, long lashes, and arching eyebrows. Fat little cheeks. I counted her perfect fingers. The tiny pink nails were razor sharp; I'd have to stay on top of them or they'd slice her tender skin. I counted her perfect toes. Her legs were bowed from living inside me. Her round belly pulled in, pushed out, pulled in, heart beating visibly inside its fragile cage. When I brought her to my breast, she latched on with the suction of an angry octopus. Gil watched me nurse. He palmed the baby's skull. "What'll we call her?" he asked. *Erin*. Because she was like my dream of Ireland. "Beautiful," said Gil. And I was overwhelmed with love and gratitude. *This man*. Who'd made a child no one could take away. Who'd made that child with me.

WITHIN A YEAR of our daughter's birth, Gil sold the phone room for next to nothing and took a job in the Bay Area hawking copy machines. It was a fresh start: I'd talked him into getting rid of the gun and separated him from his drinking buddies; he'd escaped the inexplicable collapse of his business and separated me from Mom, who increasingly found fault with him. We rented a house on Strawberry Point, a wooded peninsula eight miles across the Golden Gate Bridge from San Francisco. Each weekday morning Gil showered, shaved, and brushed his teeth. He sprayed Aqua Net over his hair. He suited up and pulled on the black Florsheim boots. He drove off, Erin and I waving good-bye from the picture window, which looked out at the bay, the water sometimes blue, sometimes green, often gray.

I SPOONED MASHED potatoes onto Gil's plate, passed him roast chicken and steamed broccoli. In LA we'd sometimes eaten Cheerios for dinner; I never thought I'd cook like Mom. "Three squares and a cot," he was saying. "Wouldn't be so bad." I gave him a look of incomprehension. He'd been grousing about his bosses ever since he got home. "San Quentin," he said, overe-nunciating. Gil's commute to East Bay took him daily past the prison, but why was he telling me this? He leaned over and kissed me. "Those guys" —he meant the inmates— "they've got a million-dollar view!"

ANOTHER THING I never thought: I'd be a stay-at-home mom. I'd worked since I was fourteen and wanted to work again. Erin at eighteen months was old enough for a sitter. "No way," said Gil. "What about school?" I asked. I dreamed of finishing my education. Gil stared at the toys on the floor, the dishes in the sink, the mop in its bucket of cold soapy water. "You can't even take care of the house, Kerry. What the fuck do you *do*?"

I HUNG OUT with the baby, that was what. Erin made things—shit, piss, vomit, and tears. She felt things—love, frustration, joy. I was her witness. She reached for shadows on the sliding-glass doors. Reached for a leaf, fingers pincering. She buried her starfish hands in the dirt. Whenever I played the piano, she crawled beneath it and danced. Every day she changed, yet the days were the same. In the bath, I plopped her between my legs and soaped her up. Silky little eel. Wrapped in towels, we migrated to the master bedroom, filled with stolen copy machines. I carried my daughter past the pile and lowered her onto the bed. We lay naked on our backs, Erin tucked against me. A smile curved around the thumb in her mouth. *Anticipation.* I lifted the sheet high with my feet and let go, dropping my legs to one side. The fabric billowed, floated, fell. Puff of sweet soapy air. A current slid over our skin as the sheet molded to noses, knees, and bellies, like the cool hands of the gods.

GIL MADE NEW friends and they were not mine. He found people to party with after work—how could I have thought he wouldn't?—and I was not invited. He drank more and I worried. "I'm not your father," he said. "I'm not an alcoholic, I can quit anytime, I just don't want to." But he came home late. And came home later. Sometimes he didn't come home at all.

HE BROUGHT ME flowers. He bought expensive gifts and took me out for special dinners and arranged fun family outings, strolling beside me with Erin perched on his shoulders. "I love you," he insisted, "I love only you." When I talked to Mom on the phone, she asked, "How are you, honey?" I said I was good. "But how are you *really*?" I'd strived to shield Gil from her criticism, but it was true that I was fine, or mostly true. Also true: I hated to be wrong. "I'm good, Mom, really," I said. "We're all good, everything's great."

HE STOOD IN his suit in the driveway at dawn, a lurid gash winking over one eye.

"Stop bawling," he said.

"You need stitches, Gil."

"Fuck that," he said.

When I asked where the car was, he pointed vaguely. "Leave me alone," he said. "The only thing I need is sleep."

I WALKED THE split road for a quarter mile before spotting a splash of maroon at the bottom of the median. The back of our car stuck up through the brush. I scrambled down the slope. The car's front end was squashed, the shattered windshield a spiderweb. It looked totaled and we had no insurance. I prayed Gil hadn't hit anyone.

Later he said, "Tree got in my way."

I was seasoning yet another chicken, darkness falling beyond the sliding glass doors. Erin played with spoons at my feet. Gil lifted the baby, cooing to make her giggle. He sidled closer. He pulled a glass from the cupboard, filled it with water, and drained it in a single swallow. I turned to face him, set a palm against the bruise on his bare chest.

"Did you fall asleep at the wheel?" I asked.

And as if I were the dimmest star in all the galaxy, he said, "Kerry, Kerry, Kerry, I was *drunk*."

GIL LOST THE job selling copy machines. He found another. Lost that one and found another. He kept me in the dark about our finances, but the house on Strawberry Point was now clearly unaffordable, so when Erin was two, we moved farther north, to a one-bedroom apartment on busy Sir Francis Drake Boulevard. It wasn't all bad. My baby grand piano fit in the living room. The Montessori school was within walking distance. In autumn, gold leaves on the trees made it look like it was raining coins. I was at long last allowed a part-time typography job. It meant the difference between making rent and eviction, and I intended to leverage that difference for freedoms.

THE KITCHEN LIGHT shined down through the glass-topped table, onto the head of a three-year-old child. Erin sat on the floor in pj's, a faded baby blanket tied around her shoulders Superman-style, and cradled an old cigar box in her lap. Stashed within it were her "continents," cardboard cutouts she'd made at preschool. She could name them all. She could recite the alphabet and knew her numbers to twenty and a few Spanish words. And she thought if she sat very still, her parents, who were fighting, would not see her. For the thousandth time, Gil said, "I don't want you hanging around with that guy!" He meant Ethan, whom I'd met in a university night class on Shakespeare's tragedies; when the class let out, Ethan always walked me to my car. I liked him, he was a friend. He worked at a tobacco shop downtown but was really a writer. I'd read a few of his stories, their surreality new to me, and thrilling.

Gil snatched at my wrist. He leaned down and said to Erin, "Come on out, monkey."

Clutching the continent box to her chest, she crawled past table legs and human legs. She stood beside her father, while, one-handed, Gil pried the box free. He stared at the faded illustration of a dark-haired woman in a white mantilla. With a forefinger, he opened the lid. The woman's image repeated on the inside, more vividly, as if containment had brought her to life. I told him again that the box was a present for Erin, and he said, "You're so fucking green." He twisted my arm, and I contorted myself to escape the pain.

EVERY NIGHT BEFORE I put Erin to bed, I chased her in circles around the apartment, she rebelling against sleep, me certain that the night world of adults and their conflicts was no place for an innocent. When I saw her flagging I reversed direction, and she ran right into my arms. And isn't that what we all want, to be pursued, and then caught?

A YOUNG COUPLE came over for dinner. The wife was a physics major at Cal, the husband a colleague of Gil's at an art gallery on Fisherman's Wharf's Pier 41. The two men sold numbered lithographs to tourists. Every few weeks, they boosted one out the back—a half-dozen LeRoy Niemans leaned against our living-room wall. Theft put food on our table, theft financed the family car, theft paid for Erin's daycare tuition and my night classes. Corruption just another cost of living. Gil and the young husband liked to go out drinking and drugging after a big sale, and sometimes the young wife phoned me at 3 a.m., imagining her husband dead in a ditch or in jail, knifed in a fight, or wrapped around another woman. I was now an old married lady of twenty-eight, my role to talk her down.

The four of us worked our way through appetizers, Caesar salad and bread, whiskey, and multiple bottles of wine. The radio played Cyndi Lauper, Bruce Springsteen, Lionel Ritchie. At midnight, Gil set four foil-wrapped baked potatoes in a bowl. He pulled sizzling T-bones from the broiler and dropped them onto a platter. The young husband gasped admiringly while his wife danced in her chair to the Pointer Sisters. Soon the tabletop looked like a crime scene, all fat and blood and bones. Knives sawed. Clink of silver against porcelain. The boys talked about their latest heist. I felt ill. "What's wrong with you?" Gil said. I shook my head. "Eat up!" he ordered. He watched me feed in a juicy morsel, then poured me more wine. The young husband, leering, told a dirty joke, and the young wife's face purpled. Her eyes behind her glasses brimmed. She leapt to her feet and clawed at her neck. I rushed around behind her and threw my arms across her chest. I closed my hand into a fist, felt for the hollow at the bottom of her ribcage, then jabbed my cupped fist upward. She grunted, a piece of steak flying from her mouth like a stone from a slingshot, while the boys stared at us glassy-eyed—comprehension seconds into the future—and laughed.

LAKE TAHOE, GIL and I in our VW bus, headed back to a friend's cabin on the California side from Harrah's casino in Stateline; this friend had stayed behind with Erin so that we could have a night out. Gil had been obnoxious at Harrah's, insulting the dealer and baiting other players. Embarrassed, I'd made a stink, and we'd left without having dinner. Now he was rip-roaring drunk and driving too fast, nursing his fury because I'd ruined his fun. We came to a stretch where darkness closed in, massive evergreens standing like sentinels. The road vanished, no way to tell where we were going or where we had been. Gil veered rightward. "Slow down," I said, and he stomped on the gas. Pine branches thumped against my window. He steered further right, and they scraped in a hard rhythm that sounded like a train. We bumped wildly along the verge. Was he trying to run me into the trees? Shrieking, I twisted in my seat. "There are better women than you!" he cried. Then he yanked the wheel left, and we were back on the road. I knelt on the seat and smacked awkwardly at his shoulders. Why? *Why?* "That's right, cunt," he said. "Go ahead. Scream."

HE GAVE ME pubic lice—itching and shame and a prescription for anti-critter shampoo. He gave me chlamydia—discharge, burning, antibiotics, and shame. He gave me chlamydia again. "You picked it up from a public toilet," he said. "*You* gave it to *me*." I sat across from him at the kitchen table, words snagged on rocks of disbelief. I wept, snot bubbling from my nose. Gil thumbed his newspaper, turning a page. I jumped up and kicked him in the shins. He remained calm as a traffic light, saying, "I love you, I love you, I love only you."

ON THE PHONE with Mom, I said: "I'm good, we're all good. Everything's great."

WHEN GIL AND I first fell in love, the age difference acted as an aphrodisiac. He'd relished shaping me to his desires, and I was happy to learn what my body was capable of. Over time, though, he turned my ardor against me. I began to use sex as appeasement or distraction. I withheld. I took care of a child, worked, and went to school; Gil demanded the cupboards be stocked, the laundry done, meals on the table, and vacuum marks in the wall-to-wall. His cheating made it hard for me to perform. Then there was my disgust at fucking him when he was soused. The smell. The careless aggression with which he forced my head or dropped his weight down. Gil took refusal as both affront and challenge. He chased me into the living room, cornered me by the couch, and pulled me down to the floor. He threw a leg over my hip and pinned me. No, I said, struggling. He grabbed a breast and twisted it. *No.* He reached down, yanked off his sneaker, and sailed it across the room. Concentrating, he tugged off a sock and stuffed it into my mouth. He tore my panties. He forced my legs apart, and pushed in, pushed in, pushed in.

SOMETIMES, AFTER A night class, I haunted the university library. I strolled through the stacks, pulling volumes. So much knowledge. So many worlds. So much beauty.

WHEN MOM LEARNED I was pregnant again, she paid for a Hawaiian vacation, a second honeymoon for Gil and me before the new baby arrived. But from the moment the plane landed on Kauai, he ranted and complained. The hotel stank, the food was awful, the beach was unswimmable, the rental car lacked air-conditioning. Lihue bored him. Worst of all, it rained and rained. "Fix it, Kerry!" he chanted, until, exhausted, I was convinced that it was my fault. On the last day, however, he announced: "Fuck it, let's drive to Hanalei."

Traveling north, the deluge became a drizzle that turned into a mist that burned away. We stopped at a vista point and stared down at fluorescent green fields carved by a river that looked like a silver sword. Gil put an arm around my shoulder. I leaned against him. There was no need to speak. Near Hanalei, we passed a pretty gothic church and a swaybacked chestnut horse in a field. The horse sheltered beneath a lone tree with a spindly trunk and a few soaked branches that thrashed in the wind. "Pull over," I said. I ran to the fence with the camera. Clouds were again gathering, darkening, descending. The air crackled and a few heavy drops fell. I lifted the viewfinder to my eye. *This horse*. Poor thing. It radiated an uncanny resignation, eyes shut, flanks quivering. It had been here forever, waiting for me to find it, waiting for me to see.

A MAN TELLS you he admires your strength but treats you as if you are weak. He says he values your smarts but smacks down any exercise of intelligence. You're beautiful, but your looks offend him. Your touch is irritating, but the absence of touch proves you are cold. He says he trusts but he isolates you. He *surveils*, checks out friends and coworkers, examines the bank statement, the phone bill, the car's mileage. He goes through your purse. Every day is like this, even when it's not. You are neither battered nor bruised, but the mind fractures. And with each passing moment you lose more of yourself, moving ever closer to being only who he says you are: a jewel, a piece of shit, a good wife, a bad wife, a good mother, and someone he'd never allow around his kids.

WHEN I WAS a little girl, I'd slept in the den, called the Red Room because of its blood-colored carpeting. This room was wallpapered in a repeating figure of men on horseback in pursuit of a fox. A rickety back door led out to our street. The key was long lost, so Mom used to plug the hole with a wad of white cotton wool. At night, from my bed, I'd watch the cotton bulge, turning into a bird that burst into the room. The bird flew all around, flapping its wings against ceiling and walls, while the three bears climbed the back of the hill, coming to eat me up. I told Gil this story not long after we met, on one of our afternoons at the conference table. He said, "No three-year-old remembers their dreams." Our faces shined up from the polished mahogany. "Don't worry, baby," he said, "I will keep you safe."

CAN WE BE known by what we love? I loved Erin and Gil and my mom. I loved the books on our shelves, and my Steinway baby grand, its polished soundboard and yellowed ivory keys. I loved Bach, Mozart, Beethoven, Chopin, how the music was a portal to another world. I loved my son and the small rectangular object that was all I had of him: a Polaroid photograph. I hid the photo in my strongbox. By this I could also be known. What about Gil? He claimed that he'd do anything for his kids, but was it true? He said he loved me, but did he? I wanted to believe that he did. He loved games, golf and poker and chess. He loved his J&B. Were there objects he cherished? Yes. His pots and pans, the antiques he nagged me to keep free of dust. He loved a blue sweater I gave him for his forty-fifth birthday. What did he hide? More than I'll ever know. That apartment on Sir Francis Drake Boulevard was a place of concealment, in every sense of the word, and while I'd never been much of a snoop, for years I'd felt a nagging absence, a shape that suggested, as with the photo of my son, a presence. And I was, God help me, afraid.

THE MARRIAGE HAD become like Schrödinger's cat, an animal trapped in a potentially lethal box, both dead and alive, its fate tethered to a random event that might or might not occur.

THIS WAS ORDINARY life.

ISN'T IT MADDENING, how incapable I was of leaving him? What would it take? Just be glad you're not me, forced by the writing to face who I was for so long, my behavior an ongoing mystery.

THE CONTRACTIONS ROLLED in, two minutes apart, no time between them to gather courage. Gil ran me a shower. He undressed me and guided me into the stall. *Contraction*. He washed my back and my hair. *Contraction*. This labor hurt so much worse than the other two. Grasping my belly, I staggered out, water sluicing from my body as if I were a mountain releasing spring streams. When the sun came up, we took Erin upstairs to a neighbor. At the hospital the doctor broke the amniotic sac with a hook. A hot gush, a hard pain. *Pushpushpushpush*. Someone settled a baby into my arms. Oh, she was perfect, with her bald head and rashy red skin. The lashless eyes struggled to open. I loved her with all my heart, as I loved Erin and my lost son. Gil watched me nurse. He set a palm on our baby's skull. "What'll we call her?" he asked. *Amy*. It means beloved. "Beautiful," Gil said. And I was overwhelmed with love and gratitude. *This man*. Who'd made another child who couldn't be taken away. Who'd made that child with me.

4

Going Up

The summer of 1973, eight full months before I met Gil, my parents rented a condominium an hour south of Los Angeles, in San Clemente, a town known for red-roofed Spanish-style architecture, rock-solid conservatism, and surf culture. Under other circumstances, I'd have been thrilled to be at the beach, but I was sixteen and four months pregnant, plagued by nausea and mortified by my popped-out belly, my unruly breasts, and pale, greasy skin; I couldn't feature lying out like other teens. In any case, the objective of this extended vacation was to hide me away from neighbors and friends until I entered St. Anne's, a Catholic maternity home, in the fall, this concealment both an extension of a certain kind of childhood and unwitting preparation for my future life.

By a weird twist of fate, St. Anne's was only a few miles from our house. Weirder still, it was where I was born, where I was given up for adoption. My parents had made it clear I could not keep my baby. In theory, I accepted that. My birth mother had gotten through this, and I would do the same. The word *mother* circled my head like a swung chain. *A mother.* That's what I would be. It was unbelievable, so I refused to believe.

Instead of joining Mom each day on the sand, I holed up in the rented condo. I closed the curtains, lazed on the couch, and escaped for hours into drugstore paperbacks. I liked to imagine myself into multigenerational tales of hardship, triumph, and love—always love. One day, I locked myself in the bathroom, cut off my long dirty-blond curls, and dyed what was left darkest brown. I stared at the stranger in the mirror, thinking with satisfaction: There! The girl who got herself into this mess is gone.

Whenever Mom let me, I cruised around in her car. I aimed first for the turnout by the pier at the north end of town, where I got out to look at the waves. Railroad tracks followed the shore, a reminder that even at the end of the world you could change direction. When a train arrived, it was felt before seen, a vibration in the soles of the feet; then came an onrush; then wind. Then I'd steer the car onto Interstate 5 and drive a thirty-mile loop: San Juan Capistrano to Oceanside. Hitting the south end of San Clemente, I'd look for Richard Nixon's estate, his Western White House.

Watergate was in the news.

My father mostly stayed up in LA; his boss was running for County Supervisor, and Daddy was busy with the campaign. Every other weekend he drove down to golf and to fight about Nixon with Mom. The three of us ate dinner in the condo's tiny kitchen, knees touching beneath the table, Mom's voice rising, and rising, until Daddy in disgust threw down his silverware. I forked in mashed potatoes, bites of hamburger and soggy green beans. Mom talked about how the president had been in San Clemente to meet with Russia's president, Leonid Brezhnev. I knew this; I'd seen it on TV. Also on TV was news that Nixon had secretly recorded all his Oval Office conversations. Was he a bad man, as Daddy maintained, or Mom's martyred Republican saint?

My father sipped his ginger ale. His gaze alighted on me and slipped away. He was ashamed of my pregnancy.

Mom, for her part, insisted on confrontation and remorse. Whenever I disappeared into my room, she followed and interrogated me. "But are you sorry?" she asked, plopping down on the bed.

She put a hand on my arm, and I shrank from her touch. "You should be sorry, Kerry." Her voice grew loud. "Why aren't you *sorry?*"

I was sorry I got caught. An unoriginal brand of remorse, but true nonetheless.

Mom asked if I prayed.

I did not pray.

In July, I felt the baby move inside me. For months I'd ignored the ache in my breasts and the pants that wouldn't zip, but I could not ignore this. *Pop pop pop.* Quickening, that's what it was called. The sensation felt like butterfly wings.

By August the butterfly had turned into a bouncing ball. My child was an acrobat.

I was astonished, and terrified.

TERRIFIED, AS WELL, of going to St. Anne's—I was certain it would be like entering jail. But when September arrived I discovered that the place felt more like a boarding school. There was a cafeteria and a chapel, a common room, and phone booths at the end of a hall. Younger girls like me attended the LA Unified satellite high school across the street, while the over-eighteens spent their days as they pleased. We were housed in doubles on the ground floor; over-eighteens lived upstairs in much larger rooms. They were adults, another species. Also upstairs was the maternity ward—labor rooms and delivery—and a nursery, everything secured behind locked double doors. Outsiders were strictly forbidden inside St. Anne's, and apart from the doctors, there were no men. Each resident was known only by first name and last initial. I was Kerry P—Kerry Phillips? Kerry Price? Kerry Peterson? My name might be any of these. It was like living inside a fairy tale: each girl entered, gestated, delivered, and departed, yet our world felt static, as if nothing would ever change. We were a sisterhood trapped in a state of suspended animation, waiting to transform. We were all the same.

I'd been a geeky kid viewed with suspicion by my peers, but at St. Anne's I made friends: Judy G, Guadalupe S, Erica M, and Cathy T. At the satellite school, we sat next to each other during typing, business math, English, and history, and when the final bell rang, walked together back to the dorm. We visited each other's rooms, did homework, played cards, and swapped maternity clothes. At dinner we claimed our table in a corner of the cafeteria and choked down mystery meat and canned peas. Most of the girls at St. Anne's hailed from greater LA, but some had traveled from California's Central Valley, from San Diego, Eureka, and San Francisco. There were also a few out-of-staters whose families sought, through distance, added protection against discovery. My roommate, Sherry E, was a fourteen-year-old farm kid from Santa Paula with corkscrew curls and a face incapable of guile. She read comic books, hoarded candy, and listened obsessively to her transistor radio.

After dinner everyone crowded into the common room, where a collection of old sofas and chairs faced a console TV as big as a car, scratchy dialogue bursting from the built-in speakers. But no one listened. Instead, we lifted up our shirts and studied our bellies. Mine was oblong, with a handy tabletop. Others were round or shaped like footballs, mammoth or delicate as fruit ripening on a tree. We were teenagers but bitched like old ladies about our swollen ankles, our constipation and heartburn. We mourned our stretch marks and varicose veins.

We told the stories of our babies' fathers: lovers, jocks, losers and creeps, jokers and grinds, a few married men. Daddy had gotten rid of mine. All it took was a phone call. I didn't know who I was angrier at: Daddy, for his uncharacteristic interference, or the boy who let himself be chased away. In the common room I made a silent vow that my next boyfriend would be someone strong, someone who knew how to fight, someone worthy of love who would love me.

In the common room we talked about sex, how it looked, how it tasted, what it sounded like, the ways it made you lose yourself and simply be. We'd all fucked at parties, indoors or out, in childhood bedrooms, in cars. It was romantic, or it wasn't. My boyfriend had refused to use a condom; it killed his feeling, he'd complained. He protested that the contraceptive foam I bought at Sav-On burned. The pill, however, was out of the question: I thought going to Planned Parenthood required my mother's permission. I got pregnant on a weekday afternoon in my own house, on the living-room sofa, the Moody Blues' "Nights in White Satin" playing on our stereo.

In and out.

We girls agreed. The dick was horrifying, relentless, divine.

A few pregnancies in that room might have been the product of rape or incest, but no one talked about that, or at least they didn't talk about it to me. At St. Anne's, the babies were everything.

We wanted them healthy, so we drank gallons of milk and took our vitamins. We saw a doctor once a month, then every two weeks, then weekly. The nurse strapped on a blood pressure cuff, drew blood, and carefully measured the height of your uterus. You listened through a stethoscope to the baby's heartbeat. That glugging thump left me ragged. In the common room I stared at my taut-skinned belly and observed the alien flurries within. Once, the baby kicked me so hard, I tried to grab its foot and hang on, but it pulled away, as if playing, leaving me empty-handed and lightheaded with fright. How would it ever get out?

Like everyone else, I crocheted.

I worked diligently on a baby blanket, fashioning yarn soft as a cloud into an intricate shell pattern, reversible pale green and cream. I made many mistakes and had to unravel the work and start again and again. The blanket would go with my baby to a new home.

Some girls knitted booties, jackets, and caps, communicating their intention to keep the child. They intended to marry the father, or not, to live with him, or with friends, or alone. Some had been disowned by their families, others would return to their parents' home. They were mothers already in ways I was not. They seemed endlessly brave, whereas I knew I was a soft, spoiled girl, even with my alcoholic father and difficult mom.

Sometimes, I ached with jealousy.

I was raised to believe that giving up a child was noble. But for most of the girls at St. Anne's, keeping their baby made them queens. Some of this was cultural; girls from Mexican-American or Black families more often found surrender unthinkable. But we all regularly saw a social worker in an office at the end of the first-floor hall; if you wanted to keep your baby, her job was to talk you out of it. With me, the task was to make sure I did not change my mind. I sweated through these appointments, tuning out the social worker while I stared at the locked file cabinets along the back wall. What paperwork had been stored there, and how far back did it go? Was my birth mother in those cabinets, filed under a name I'd never known?

When I was a child, my parents made a myth of my adoption: a midnight summons, a frantic drive down sleeping city streets. A woman in white led them along a corridor and into a room filled with bassinets. Up and down the aisles they went, stopping to examine every newborn. But none of the babies seemed right. When they came to the last bassinet, they peered down at a tiny girl with no hair, no eyebrows, and a rashy red face. The baby squalled. Beaming, they turned to the woman in white.

We'll take that one.

You were chosen, they told me.

I accepted this. In my parents' story the birth mother was nowhere to be found, adoption a rescue rather than a wound from which mother and child never entirely recovered.

I told no one I'd been born at St. Anne's. It was a secret I felt obligated to keep. But as the weeks passed I thought with increasing frequency about the woman who gave me away. How she'd walked these same halls, how she'd sat in the cafeteria and ate the same meals. How she'd made me from her body only to let me go. In this way, we were the same. And I wondered: Why was I musical, when Mom and Daddy were not? Why was I unathletic, when they enjoyed sports? I was oversensitive and, according to Mom, a daydreamer who lacked common sense. Was the woman who bore me the same? Where did she live now, and did she have a family? The most burning question: Why didn't she want me?

"It's best for the baby," the social worker said flatly. "And for you."

If I gave my child away, what would happen to me?

Going up. That's what we younger girls called it, giving birth on the second floor. As if it were an ascension to another realm, where the waiting would end and we'd be, at long last, transformed.

THE FIRST TIME Mom brought me home for a weekend visit, she picked me up on a Friday after work. I watched for her from the reception area, my breath catching when her car pulled into the lot. Every Sunday we talked on the phone, but I hadn't seen her in weeks. She looked like a stranger, younger, her expression uncertain in a way I'd never seen.

I hurried out to the car, but getting in I felt self-conscious, my belly so much larger now. Mom slanted herself sideways and kissed my cheek. "Ready?" she asked. "Ready," I agreed. She accelerated into the street. I rolled down my window and stuck my head out into the wind like a happy dog.

We shopped for groceries at an unfamiliar supermarket in Koreatown; I was, as ever, hiding. Mom pushed the cart while I picked out fruit and cereal. We loaded up on vegetables, chicken, and beef.

At the bottom of our hill, I slunk down in my seat—the invisible girl. At the top, Mom hit the clicker for the garage. The door rattled up, we pulled in, the door rattled down. We snuck around back to the kitchen.

I ate my way through the weekend. Mom and I companionably watched TV. On Sunday we attended church at a different parish, while Daddy was out working on the campaign. Avoiding him was easy.

That evening, when Mom returned me to St. Anne's, I found my roommate Sherry E's bed stripped, her side of the closet emptied. She was supposed to go home for the weekend, too. Maybe she'd gone up, I thought. But her due date was three months away. The baby would be premature.

In the cafeteria, Erika M told me Sherry's boyfriend brought her back to St. Anne's before they'd gone forty miles: Sherry had hemorrhaged in the car. The rumor was that they'd pulled over to have sex, which brought on labor. The boyfriend ran into reception with his girl in his arms, her white pants stained red, her white T-shirt stained red, blood all over his hands. They rushed Sherry upstairs for an emergency Caesarian, but the baby was stillborn.

Sherry stayed on the ward for several days, but they wouldn't let me see her, and I was at school when she left. I begged the office for her phone number, but they refused. I didn't even know her last name. I called Mom, crying, from the booth in the hall. The next day, she came to collect me.

She wanted me to go to confession, so she drove us downtown to Queen of Angels church on Main—I was due in less than a month, and Mom was afraid I'd die in childbirth with a mortal sin on my soul. She couldn't quite bring herself to say I'd go directly to hell, but I knew what she felt. She worked for the Right to Life League of Southern California. She'd made me go on their marches. She saw the Supreme Court's recent decision on *Roe v. Wade* as akin to the Holocaust. Nothing excused abortion, not rape, not incest, not the mother's life. If mine were endangered during childbirth, I knew she'd choose the baby. I wanted to ask how she could do that but was afraid of what she would say.

Inside the darkened church people clustered near the confessional, where a line had formed. Mom herded me into a pew. You had to examine your soul in advance, teasing out sins via a review of the Ten Commandments. Mine were the usual. Lies, disrespecting my parents, taking the Lord's name in vain. The big one, the reason why we were here, fell under the Sixth Commandment: impure thoughts and deeds.

Mom elbowed me and I exited the pew. When my turn in line came, I swept aside a velvet curtain and entered. I dropped to my knees. A priest sat in shadow on the other side of the screen. I murmured my opening lines. *Bless me, Father, for I have sinned. My last confession was . . .*

Eventually, I got to the point.

"What sorts of impure deeds, missy?" the priest asked. "Do you touch yourself?"

Of course I did, but this wasn't the sin I didn't want to confess.

"I'm pregnant," I blurted.

The priest shifted, his robes rustling. "You've had . . . sexual intercourse?"

Obviously. I would not say it.

The priest sighed. "How old are you, missy?"

"Sixteen."

"Sixteen! And will you be getting married?"

"No," I said.

"You're in a fix, aren't you?"

I'd only done what humans were designed for, I thought resentfully. And now I had life in me.

The priest wanted to know how many times. I told him I didn't remember, but this was a lie. I remembered them all.

My belly hardened suddenly, a Braxton-Hicks contraction. My cervix zinged. Over the past week my womb had dropped, the baby's head snugged tightly into my pelvic girdle and pressing down. The kicking had mostly stopped. In the confessional's stillness, I pictured the child listening.

"God sees you," the priest said. "He knows what you've done. He knows what you are."

I wrapped my arms around my belly. I didn't want the baby to hear. This priest was only a man. He didn't know me.

He assigned me a penance, and I said the Act of Contrition. Freed, I stumbled out of the confessional. I made another vow: I would never again confess to a man. When I slid into the pew next to Mom, she leaned over and whispered, "I feel so much better, Kerry. Don't you?"

For once, we agreed.

ON THANKSGIVING MORNING, Mom collected me from St. Anne's for the third time. We usually spent the holiday at my aunt and uncle's house in La Cañada, but not this year. Mom was cooking prime rib for just the three of us, rather than turkey. Prime rib was my favorite. We'd have mashed potatoes and creamed spinach, too, and for dessert, pumpkin pie with Cool Whip.

At four o'clock, we gathered at the table. Mom asked me to say grace. We dug in. There was little conversation, for which I was grateful. The food tasted otherworldly delicious and I stuffed myself, my belly filling and tightening until I could hardly move. Afterward, Daddy settled in the living room to watch football, while Mom and I did the dishes. I lumbered from table to sink, from countertop to cupboard, while Mom told a story I'd always taken delight in, how when she was five, her older sister, who was babysitting her, ditched her on the streets of New York. Amazing to picture my competent, no-nonsense mother lost and alone. The story had a happy ending of sorts, with a kind policeman, and ice cream, and a whipping for my Aunt Kathleen.

We joined Daddy in the living room, where he'd laid a crackling fire. He sat in his blue easy chair; Mom sat in hers. I arranged myself cross-legged in a corner of the couch, hands clasped over my enormity. I ignored the TV and stared into the fire. The flames licked orange and blue. Sparks flew like Tinkerbell up the chimney.

Over and over my belly hardened. More Braxton-Hicks contractions, I assumed, no point in mentioning them. The football game ended and some program began. And another. Mom got up and turned off the TV, and we all went to bed.

I dreamed I was holding a seashell to my eye, examining its pink and gray whorls. I stood underneath a pier, gaping at the people above me who strolled the boards. The ocean looked liverish, a dark line lifting at the horizon. I had an urge to pee, but there were snakes all over my bedroom floor.

I woke up cramping—it felt like the worst period pain. In the bathroom, I lifted my nightgown and pulled down my panties. A mucosy glop of blood stained my underwear.

This must be it, I thought.

Instead of waking Mom, I returned to the living room. The

fire's embers glowed. On the other side of our picture window, the night sky was a strange shade of lavender. I put a couple of logs on and resumed my spot on the couch, and there I sat until dawn, timing my pains. They hurt, but were nowhere near unbearable.

This was it. This was really it.

When the sun was full up, I crept into my parents' room. In sleep, they looked defenseless. Mom's eyes popped open—she'd sensed my presence.

"What," she said.

"The baby's coming."

She shook Daddy, told him she was taking me to the hospital. She dressed quickly, then lit a cigarette, hands shaking, then left it to burn in an ashtray. She drove me to St. Anne's, praying aloud and white-knuckling the steering wheel all the way.

Hail Mary full of grace, the Lord is with thee . . .

The nun in reception led us upstairs. Mom and I waited outside the locked ward until a nurse approached and hit a button and the doors swung open. Mom hugged me goodbye. I clung to her. She whispered into my ear, but I did not catch the words, and so I would not remember them. The nurse said something—I had to go on alone.

In the labor room, the nurse told me to undress and put on a gown, to climb onto the hospital bed and open my legs. Cold fingers poked and probed. A pain began, and I yelped. The nurse withdrew her hand. "You're nowhere near ready yet, dear." She dropped two huge white pills into my fist and handed me a glass of water. With a razor she scraped the hair from my pubis, then turned me onto my side and administered a warm enema. For a moment I dozed. When I came to, I was alone, groggy and nauseated, the need to shit overwhelming. I climbed out of bed and fell onto the floor, then crawled to the bathroom. I pulled myself up onto the toilet. The walls slanted and bulged and a kind of poison poured out of me. I shivered uncontrollably and vomited onto the tile. A tidal wave of pain arrived. I heard a scream. I thought the sound came from me, then realized it was some other girl in some other room who was also laboring.

The pain built again.

The nurse found me on the bathroom floor. I snarled when she touched me. She hauled me up as the contraction crested and guided me to the bed. She left the room, returned, left again. I wept. I needed my mother—where was my mother? Why wasn't she here? The contractions lurched onward, closer together, bands of ever-tightening fire. My belly rose up and out, the skin so strained I was sure it would split. I felt a frantic downward-grinding sensation along with pressure on my rectum. Panting, I bucked to get away from the pain. The nurse materialized by the side of the bed.

"I can't," I said. She inserted a hand inside me, and *uh uh,* I wanted to push more than I'd ever wanted to do anything. *Pushpushpushpush.*

"Try to hold back," the nurse advised.

She wheeled the bed into the delivery room.

Movement, bright light, arctic air.

Someone lifted me onto a table and rolled me. A needle pierced the skin over my lower spine. I grunted as another contraction arrived. All at once the anesthetic kicked in, and the agony lifted.

Bliss.

A blunt tug, followed by a metallic clang, followed by a sound like a song on a record played at too high a speed. Silence. The sound came again. It was my baby crying. Someone announced that I'd had a boy, and I laughed, dazzled. Someone dipped the child in my direction before whisking him away. Two hard pushes on my belly and the placenta slipped into a pan. The doctor bent to sew up the episiotomy.

The nurse wheeled me back into the hallway. It felt like a *ride.*

Just before turning into a recovery room, I glanced at the double doors. There, framed in the window, were smiling faces, Guadalupe S and Judy G. They must've heard I'd gone up. They grinned and waved. I lifted and twisted my torso, grinning back like a maniac, and waved. You weren't supposed to do that after a spinal, I'd heard, it could leave you paralyzed, that's what all the girls said. I didn't care. I was higher than high, my joy uncontainable.

I'd had a baby. A baby, a baby. A boy.

THREE DAYS LATER I went home. And there, surrounded by all that was familiar, I succumbed to grief. I couldn't sit with my parents. I was unable to eat. I felt like I had a raging fever. The thermometer read as normal, but I was not normal. At night I dreamed of drowning in an inch of water, or searching through a drawer for lost keys. I felt my baby everywhere and nowhere, just out of reach.

Daddy wasn't around much, but Mom stayed home from work for two weeks. She would not leave me be. She hovered, nervous I'd renege on giving up the baby. She offered to drive me to the adoption agency to sign the papers. Tomorrow, I said. Don't take too long, she said, before returning, defeated, to the Right to Life League.

I didn't know what to do with myself—I wouldn't start at the new high school until next year. I hadn't seen my friend Pam in ages—I could call her up and invite her over. And we'd . . . what? Eat Kraft macaroni and cheese? Watch *All My Children*? Pore over the latest fashions in *Seventeen*? Or I could walk down the hill to Sunset Boulevard and get on a bus and escape. But there was no escape. Daydreaming was a distraction, and distraction a sin. So I kept to the house, restless, and paralyzed.

Mornings, once Mom and Daddy left, I brought my radio into the bathroom, plugged it in by the sink, and cranked up the volume so I could hear the music over water thundering into the tub.

Stretched out, I confronted my lonely-looking body. Who did it belong to now? Not me. And not the baby. My belly was still mounded where my child had so recently been. In the hospital they'd given me a shot to dry up my milk, but my breasts still felt hard, and my nipples leaked grudgingly. I bled scarlet threads that wound out into the water from between my thighs. When the tub cooled, I drained it a bit before blasting the hot again. On the radio songs came and went. Diana Ross sang as if directly to me, about mountains and rivers that could never get in love's way.

I was my son's mother. That was a fact forever.

But he deserved a mother and a father. But then his mother would never be me.

What made a mother?

My last day on the maternity ward, the social worker told me that my son's new parents were good Catholics, the father a businessman, the wife a stay-at-home mom. They had another adopted child, a boy who'd just turned three. My son would have a brother.

Who were these people? How did they think, what did they want, how did they love? Why would I ever relinquish my son to their care?

I didn't know what to do.

Then one morning I came upon my father by the front door, sprawled on the carpet as if murdered. His eyelids stood at half-mast, his legs bent at an awkward angle. He'd flung an arm to one side. His open robe exposed his skinny white legs. When he was a boy, Daddy's left calf had been mangled in a trolley accident, so he never wore shorts, and the scar was seldom displayed. It looked so deeply purpled I feared a fresh injury. Oh, he's had a heart attack! I thought. I ran to him, knelt close, then reared back at the fumes.

"Goddamn it," I said.

Daddy coughed, a sound like charcoal scraped from a grill. He struggled to open his eyes. Caught up in my own misery, I'd missed how one beer had turned into a six-pack, then into whiskey. He was on a binge.

His fine black hair fell over his brow. He stuck out his bottom lip and blew the strands away. "I need a bottle," he rasped. "Take my car and drive down the hill and get me one."

I shook my head. I couldn't legally buy him liquor, even if I wanted to. Which I didn't.

He clawed at my arm. "I helped you when you were in need."

Disgusted, I scrambled to my feet. How, exactly, had he helped—by hiding me in San Clemente? By banishing me to St. Anne's? By insisting I give up my son?

What kind of man was he?

What made a father?

I decided I'd never bring a baby into this house; I would give my son to the nice Catholic family and never see him again. The finality of this decision felt like tying myself to train tracks. All I could do was wait for the train.

I stared down at my father. My whole life, he'd been a drunk. I had no memory of it ever being otherwise.

His eyes pleaded up at me. He looked petrified.

What I didn't know was that, while I was at St. Anne's, Daddy had been diagnosed with cancer of the larynx. In January, not long after I entered John Marshall High, he'd go into the hospital to have his larynx removed.

In February, I'd notice in the guidance counselor's office an index card thumbtacked to a bulletin board. *Office supply company seeks part-time secretary.* Soon I'd sit at a conference table with my boss. I'd spend a night in Las Vegas with a man twice my age, seduced by a lover who assured me that, for his kids, he'd do anything.

Daddy's cancer was supposed to be one of the good ones, cleanly defined and easily removed, but errant cells had already spread to his lymph nodes. From there they made their way to his lungs. Within a year he was gone. At the funeral mass, I stood dry-eyed in the pew; I wanted to cry, but the tears wouldn't come.

I left my father alone in the entry. I had no room in my heart.

ON MY LAST day on the maternity ward at St. Anne's, just before Mom arrived to bring me home, I was granted an hour alone with my son.

A nurse led me into a small room adjacent to the nursery. She gestured at a rocking chair, and I sat. After she left, I watched the wall clock. My pulse kept time with the second hand, *tick tick tick.* Seconds became minutes. Six passed before the nurse returned.

"Are you ready?" she asked.

I nodded.

She settled the baby in the crook of my arm. The weight of him. His warmth like a small fire. I bent to smell the top of his head.

The nurse said, "You have to support it."

"I *know.*"

The nurse lingered.

Go away, I thought fiercely. She must have felt it, because she turned on her heel. The door clicked shut behind her.

Like mothers everywhere, I counted my son's fingers. I undid the plain blue blanket and counted his toes. I wished I could wrap him in the one I'd crocheted in the common room. All my tenderness was in it. But the blanket sat in a box at the adoption agency.

Holding him, he'd felt solid as a little football. The left side of his head was mashed from the forceps used to pull him out of me, but his hair, thick and unruly, covered the dent. That hair was gold. Not brown, not blond—gold.

I touched the soft spot on his skull, felt the trembling beat of his pulse. The baby gazed up at me with unfocused eyes.

Oh, I recognized him.

The door opened. The nurse came in and I tightened my hold.

"It's time," she said.

I thought I might faint. But fainting was weak. I wouldn't give this woman the satisfaction.

"Are you ready?" she asked.

I was not ready. I would never be ready. I refused to look up.

My hands tingled. Rockets were going off in my chest. I'd always wanted to be someone else, and now I was: a mother who surrenders her son. I'd known this moment was coming but not what I'd feel.

"It's time," she said again.

This child. I memorized his face.

The nurse leaned over us. "You'll have others," she said, and lifted him from my arms.

5

Two Stories

I am going to tell you two stories. One is true, the other a lie, and not necessarily in that order.

STORY 1

I sat alone at the kitchen table. The windows were black, the trees in the yard indistinguishable from the sky. The apartment was quiet, my four-year-old daughter asleep in her bed. The baby due in a month rested inside me. My eyes were tired, and I had to tilt the book in my hand to escape the glare from the overhead light. Across from me a newspaper lay open on the tabletop. My husband was in the bathroom off the kitchen and had been for some time. He'd started drinking before dinner, and it occurred to me that he'd taken the glass in there with him, because the sweat rings on the newspaper had dried. I put the book down and called his name, but he didn't answer.

I got up and went into the hall and loitered outside the closed bathroom door. I gave a tentative rap, and tried the handle. *Locked.* And instantly I was furious, sure he'd shut himself up to do drugs, to snort cocaine, or crank, or whatever it was he'd hidden away.

"Open it!" I pounded on the door. "Fucking open it!"

He did, unexpectedly, and I squeezed inside. I wedged my pregnant bulk into a corner. Our bathroom was tiny: a narrow shower, a cabinet sink, a medicine chest hung too high on the wall. In this tight space my husband smelled sour. He stood smirking at himself in the mirror, leaning in to his reflection. He dropped his jaw to inspect his molars. The metal clasps of his dental bridge shined— we were together for years before I learned that he had a bridge. How do you kiss a man and never notice?

The gun at his temple wobbled.

"I could be gone," he said. "Just like that."

My throat constricted. I started to cry.

He turned and pointed the gun at my belly. His wrist shook as if the weapon was too heavy to hold.

"Stop sobbing," he said. "It isn't loaded."

I reached out and smacked at his arm. It jerked and the gun went off in the sink. The sound deafened me. There was a sharp smell, a powdery cloud. My husband looked surprised, and then he looked . . . *interested*. He opened his mouth to speak but I couldn't hear him, not a single word.

STORY 2

It was the summer of 1968. I was twelve and my brother Mick had just turned nine. We lived with our parents in the Los Feliz neighborhood of Los Angeles, on a street called Waverly Drive. It was a solidly middle-class area, with trees and lawns and 1920s-era homes, but there were no other children on the block to play with and we were often alone. My brother was, as Mom said, young for his age—he suffered from ants in the pants, and still wet the bed— and he wasn't allowed out in front of the house unless I was with him.

That August, Sharon Tate, the pregnant wife of director Roman Polanski, along with three of her friends and a young man visiting the caretaker, were murdered at a house in Beverly Hills. The next night Rosemary and Leno LaBianca were killed. The LaBiancas also lived on Waverly Drive, across the street and three doors down from our family. My parents knew them to say hello to, but to me and to Mick they were middle-aged shadows, all but invisible.

For days cops and reporters swarmed the area, which was scary but also exciting. Mick and I were told to stay inside. Things calmed down eventually, but we never did get an explanation of what had happened. I learned what I could by eavesdropping on adults, from the news on TV, and once school started, from playground gossip, some of which was contradictory, some of which I knew to be false: Leno LaBianca owed the Mafia money; Roman Polanski had had his wife killed; the murders were related, or else the LaBiancas were a copycat crime. I knew the word *PiG* had been scrawled in blood on the front door at Sharon Tate's house, *Death to Pigs* on the wall in the LaBiancas' living room. None of it made any sense.

One Sunday in mid-December, a photograph of Charles Manson appeared on the front page of the *Los Angeles Times*. Due to be released from custody for an entirely different crime, he'd been named by a jailhouse snitch as the perpetrator of the summer's murders.

Mick and I lounged on the living room floor, the *Times* spread all around us. Mick lay on his stomach, chin propped in his hands. He stared at Manson's photo, the weird eyes, the stringy long hair. He recognized this guy, he said; he'd seen him on our block a day or two before the killings, sitting with some girls in a car at the foot of the LaBiancas' driveway. Manson had called him over to the driver's side window.

"He told me a joke," Mick said.

"He did not," I said, the response automatic, because my brother was a liar. He lied to get out of trouble; he lied to make himself important; he lied, sometimes, to be loved.

"Knock knock," Mick said.

"Who's there?" Another automatic response. Because if some-one started a knock-knock joke, you had to complete it.

"Leno."

"Leno who?"

"Leno little closer. I want to tell you a secret."

"That never happened," I said.

Mick shrugged. "How do you know? You weren't there."

LIKE MANY WRITERS, I also teach, and I often begin a workshop with these stories, told more or less as written here and prefaced identically: *One is true, the other a lie, and not necessarily in that order.* I keep my tone and expression neutral throughout, hands folded and body still. When finished, I ask the students to vote for the narrative that seems most likely true. We then discuss why they've chosen as they have.

Someone might see the Manson story as false, because it's stated up front that the younger brother wasn't allowed to play outside alone. Another counters that Mick's defiance makes it more real. Someone else finds it far-fetched that a pregnant woman would remain in a bathroom with a man holding a gun. We talk about exposition, the information needed to understand the action, and how sensory details make a story come alive. We talk about point of view, and what it means to put words in a character's mouth. I ask how their perception of what happened might change if the stories were switched from first person to third. *She sat alone at the kitchen table.*

By this time I've usually coughed up the truth. The gun story, I say, that's the one that happened to me. Which means the other must be a lie. And so it is.

Everything I know about the events of August 8–9, 1969, comes from what I've read in books and articles or seen in documentary films. Like the girl in my story, I was twelve when the murders occurred, just beginning to see the world on my own terms. But I don't have a younger brother; I have no siblings. And my family never lived on Waverly Drive.

I first encountered *Helter Skelter,* Vincent Bugliosi's classic account of the case, in 1974, not long after I started working for Gil. My father had received the hardback as a Christmas present; when he went into the hospital for his laryngectomy, he'd left it behind. I'd picked the book up, drawn, as were so many others, by the guilty thrill of touching evil. Manson was a real live bogeyman, his followers mostly spooky young women from ordinary middle-class families. He swept them up at just the right age and time, and he convinced those girls to let him speak for them, to see him as something other than what he was: a man who could turn their alienation to his own purposes. They were ripe for a con he'd built over years spent in prison, the psychology part L. Ron Hubbard, part Dale Carnegie: *Control the mark by making her feel important. Let her believe your ideas are hers. Talk about what she wants and how to get it.* Manson gave his followers a new family. He gave them new names. He told them he was their savior and they his chosen people. And they became killers for him. What in their lives had made them so susceptible?

Later, when all were caught, Manson's girls still believed. In their jail cells they carved swastikas into their foreheads, as he had, and they walked to court arm in arm, singing, telling anyone who would listen, *Charlie is love.*

At seventeen I'd been repulsed, but now they remind me of me. That's the uneasy truth hiding inside the second story, the one that is a lie.

Gil, of course, was no mass murderer, whatever else he may have done. And I was no groupie. I was, however, vulnerable. Gil, like Charlie Manson, could smell it. Like Manson, he was a salesman to the core, an unrepentant petty criminal, a charismatic liar who lived inside his own reality. His gift lay in the ability to make you feel important, and beloved, and seen. In return, most people saw him as he saw himself: a good father, a good husband, a good man. Maybe Gil had it in him to be good. Or maybe it was only the performance of goodness.

In class, every once in a while, someone will return to the first story. "What happened next?" they'll ask. "To the husband, and the children. And *you*. What happened to you?"

"I divorced him," I say. "It was a long time ago, I was another person then." And it's true, we did divorce, and I am not who I once was. But the statement is misleading. Two years passed before I left Gil. He'd pointed that gun at my pregnant belly, and I'd failed to scoop up my daughter and run.

That failure, the shame of it, has everything to do with who I am.

Erin slept through the gunshot—I think she did. Possibly, it entered her dreams, a poke to the solar plexus, a flash of light behind her closed lids. But when I checked on her, her breathing was even, her chest rising and falling under the sheet. I knelt by the bed and kissed her hot brow. She smelled musty, a little doughy, as children who have not had a bath before going to bed do. I waited for what would come next, but there was nothing. No stomp of footsteps in the apartment upstairs, no lights burning in the building next door, no sirens wailing out in the street. The police did not break down our door. How could that be? Gil had shot a hole in the sink.

From the bedroom I heard the freezer door open, the clink of ice cubes falling into a glass. I heard the scrape of chair legs, Gil seating himself at the kitchen table. *It was late, the windows were black, the trees in the yard indistinguishable from the sky.* I dragged a blanket and pillow from our bed, crept to the living room, and curled up on the couch. I held my breath, listening. My heart was beating too fast, the baby pressed up under my ribs. Why did Gil still have that gun? Years ago, he'd promised to get rid of it, and I'd believed him; instead, he'd hidden it.

I had to leave. My mind raced—how to get out, *how*? what could I do? where could we go? would he allow it?—and I was sure I wouldn't sleep. But I did. And in the morning the sun came up, as it does, and Gil seemed his usual self, no worse for the night's wear, chipper even, bacon and eggs on the stove, and coffee brewing, our girl seated at the glass-topped table, bare feet swinging, gabbing as he cooked her breakfast. Gil smiled broadly, listening to his child as if she were the most compelling person on earth.

And I remember thinking, He'll look at me now, his expression full of remorse. *It was an accident. I didn't know the gun was loaded. I'd never hurt you.* Or maybe he'd be defiant and cruelly offhand, saying tersely, *You're fine.* Maybe he'd bluff. *Where do you get this shit, baby? You're off your rocker. It was all a dream.*

I'd have found that last scenario consoling. If I'd dreamed it, it couldn't be real. And if it wasn't real, I'd never have to tell anyone. And if I never told anyone, I would not have to leave.

You can hold conflicting ideas in your head, but it makes you crazy.

I grasped my belly, huge with our child.

And I thought, No one has been hurt, after all. No one is perfect, no marriage is perfect, there are always shadows.

The truth was, I still loved Gil then. We'd met when I was so young. We'd been together so long. I couldn't imagine life without him. So I stayed.

THERE WAS A game I used to play as a kid. I'd hide a bit of treasure somewhere in the house—a piece of my mother's costume jewelry, a soft white slice of Wonder Bread—then sit at the dining room table and draw myself a map. I'd put in lots of detail, furniture and people, markers and clues, everything needed to find the treasure. And I'd march around chanting, "According, according, according to the *map!*" The success of this game, and my pleasure in it, depended on pretending not to know what I clearly did know.

But the body's a snitch. Liars scratch or fidget or hold themselves unnaturally still. They look away, or else too directly into your eyes. A polygraph measures heartbeat and breathing, rising blood pressure, and sweat, but it can't measure the source of the stress. Is it the lie, or the fear of being thought a liar? Can you lie to yourself? Can you really? With an fMRI, neuroscientists map blood flow to the brain. Lie, and areas associated with conflict and emotion light up. The brain must stop itself from telling the truth before it can formulate an alternative reality. The scan glows red. The task literally generates heat.

GIL REPAIRED THE hole in the sink, then smoothed a thin layer of epoxy over the bowl, leaving only the barest rim of its original surface. The bullet was embedded into the sink's underside. There it stayed. If you didn't know where to look, you'd never see.

Again, he promised to get rid of the gun. Again, I chose to believe him. And when, after Amy was born, I saw that he loved her as he loved Erin, and somehow, I just . . . forgot. Amy crawled, she spoke her first words, she took her first steps. Our daughters grew. Such an ordinary miracle. Gil and I fought and made up, fought and made up. But he was becoming angrier, more vengeful, impulsive, and unpredictable. And I retreated, convinced it was what I deserved.

This was ordinary life.

What would it take for me to leave him?

What would it take?

HE HUSTLED ME across the kitchen, shoved me into the broom closet, and threw shut the bolt. He slapped the outside of the door, a friendly slap.

"Now you can think—isn't that what you wanted, baby, time to *think*?"

Sound of footsteps moving away. The kitchen door slammed. I shouted after him, but he was on his way to the car, where the girls were waiting. We'd planned to bring them into the city for the day— Erin was now a stubborn six and Amy a terrible two, and Gil needed me, he couldn't leave without me. Yet he had. I didn't understand. What did I do? Something, or nothing. "Help!" I shouted. Were our upstairs neighbors home? "Help! Help!" Nothing. The broom closet was dark, stuffy and hot, crowded with cleaning and painting supplies. There was barely enough room to rotate in place. I didn't know what to do. The water heater kicked off. The water heater kicked on. Roaring hot breath of a lion, the pilot light licking blue fire. Who stored chemicals near a gas appliance? The whole building could blow. Sweating, I extricated a broom and jammed the handle at where I thought the bolt was, trying to knock it loose. No good. I set the broomstick aside and rammed my shoulder into the door. No good. The water heater kicked off. I dumped plastic bags from a bucket, turned it over, and sat. Okay, I'd *think*. I never had time to think. That's what I told Gil when he was after me, when he was gaslighting or demanding love or criticizing. But I didn't think—I dozed. When the water heater kicked on, I awakened with a start. My bladder ached, the urgency made worse by a torrent of tears. Stop crying!, I ordered myself. Crying gets you nowhere. Think of the girls. What are they doing right now? Eating pastries on Union Street? Climbing up to Coit Tower? What has Gil told them about why I'm not with them? Don't think about how much you have to pee. But I couldn't hold it any longer, so I flipped the bucket and squatted. Now the closet stank. How long would he leave me in here? Why hadn't I fought him? What was that sound? *Rain.*

And I remembered the horse I'd met on our trip to Kauai, standing in its field, so patiently enduring the rain. My pulse galloped. I couldn't fight, I couldn't flee. And now I shook all over, engaged in the struggle of maintaining the lie that Gil and I were a normal couple who'd made for their children a loving family.

The water heater kicked on. The water heater kicked off. What was that sound? The kitchen door opening? Footsteps, and a fluty piping: "Where's Mommy?" *Amy.* I wanted to call out to her, but the words wouldn't come. Gil said playfully, "Mommy's hiding! Why don't you look?" The girls were running through the apartment, Erin singing, "Where oh where can Mommy be?"

"Check behind the sofa," Gil said, his voice right outside the closet. Please, I thought. Please. "Check under the bed," he said.

"Mommy?"

Gil slid open the lock. He swung the door and reached in to grab me. He yanked me out, and I fell against him before jerking away. The girls buzzed around us, Erin yelling, "Daddy found you!" Flailing, I clawed at her jacket, which was slick with rain. She wrapped her arms around my waist. Amy wrapped her arms around my leg. I dragged them a few steps away from Gil. I felt him behind me, willing me to turn. Raindrops beat against the window, like pebbles thrown to catch my attention. I looked over a shoulder at Gil. His sweater, beaded with water, was zipped to the neck. He had one hand cozily buried in a pocket. He absorbed my scrutiny, his brow untroubled.

"You have a good think?" he asked, all innocence.

He wasn't drunk, he wasn't high, he wasn't angry. He had a new job that he liked and was making money. We'd been in a good phase for weeks.

The truth landed like a blow. He didn't love me.

A more devastating truth stood beside that one, seeking shelter where there was none, like that Hawaiian horse in the rain.

Look at it, Kerry.

Look at it.

I no longer loved him.

6

Burning

There is a photo of Vinnie and me taken in 1980 at the reception of my wedding to Gil, which was held on the grounds of the old Canfield-Moreno estate in LA, right across the street from Mom's. We had round tables set about a wide lawn, a buffet of Polynesian food, and an open bar stocked with Chilean champagne. A string quartet played the guests in. During the meal mariachis wove through the tables. After the cake was served, a wedding band played. A week of rain had scrubbed the sky to a celestial blue, the San Gabriel Mountains sharply visible, the top of Mount Baldy covered in snow, but all afternoon a bank of charcoal-colored clouds gathered to the north. People noted how dark they were, how threatening, what a miracle it was that somebody somewhere kept them at bay.

Vinnie and I stood at the edge of the portable dance floor.

We were eight years away from falling in love, but Vinnie was already an old friend; he'd worked briefly for Gil, one of his ubiquitous actor-slash-phone-salesmen. I found him appealingly soft-spoken, smart but not show-offy, polite but not smarmy, sexy but seemingly unaware. I liked him very much, but I did not think of him as someone for me.

In the photo my hair looks unruly under its flowery crown, perhaps from dancing. My face is flushed, also perhaps from dancing. My nose is crinkled, my mouth open—the photographer catching me midsentence. Vinnie's tie is loose, the top button of his shirt undone. We face each other, inches apart, and while I don't remember the subject of our conversation, I do remember that the strapless satin rectangle I wore, a modest foundation I'd sewn for under my dress, was slipping. I remember reaching into the bodice to tug at it, hoping to prevent a breast from popping free. I remember standing in one spot so long my stilettos sank into the grass.

I lost my balance. My arms windmilled to head off a fall. Vinnie caught me. Gil stood at the bar, leaning back on one elbow, staring at us. Reflexively, I reached into the bodice again, and Gil raised his champagne glass. His lips moved. I couldn't hear him, but I knew what he was saying. *Baby, this one's for you.*

I WAS A faithful girlfriend and wife for fourteen years and could not have imagined being the sort of woman who escapes a bad marriage with another man waiting in the wings, every aspect of the situation made worse because the man has a wife.

THE SPRING OF 1988, Gil and I drove down to LA on business. We brought the girls with us; we wanted to take them to Disneyland. Mom had just moved to a small town outside San Diego, so we stayed with Vinnie and his then wife in West Hollywood. One night, both unable to sleep, Vinnie and I took a walk while everyone else was in bed. The streets were quiet. Night flowers released their perfume. There was no moon. We talked in fits and starts, and I was struck, as I so often was, by Vinnie's gentleness. We'd been platonic familiars for years—I'd known him almost as long as I'd known Gil, and because we'd never had cause to hide them, we were well aware of each other's weaknesses. On Melrose Avenue we glided from shop window to shop window, cheek to cheek as we tried to see in. We didn't speak about how unhappy we were, though our unhappiness was undeniable. We walked close, and then closer, physical proximity like a drug. I felt breathless and buoyant, sober and giddy and alive. When Vinnie reached for me, I pressed myself into his warmth. We kissed, and there was such promise in it. In that moment we settled things between us. It would be months before we slept together—we lived four hundred miles apart, we were both married, and I was a mom—but when we did, it felt like the embodiment of true love. It hit me like a tsunami. A line of sensual feeling, and of hope, rose on the horizon, and then the wave rushed in, engulfing everything.

We spent time in motels, hungry, tender, obsessed. Burning. We talked on the phone, sometimes for hours. Life went on as usual around us and we were careless in the midst of it, as if wanting to be caught. But we were not caught.

We arranged an illicit weekend in Lake Tahoe, where we walked around Harrah's for a half hour before growing distracted and going back to our room. We smoked a little pot and listened to music and made love. In the morning we drove the road where I believed Gil had tried to run me into the trees, though that now seemed a mirage. We ate in a restaurant right on the highway, running to it from the car, holding hands in broad daylight. Our lives could be like this, we thought, easy and free. The next day, our last in Tahoe, we visited the property where in *Godfather II* Michael sends his brother Fredo to his death on a boat for betraying him. The house sat behind gated walls, but from an easement to the south you could see the back side, a sweep of lawn leading down to a pier. An old man who was fishing asked if we were on our honeymoon. We looked at each other and said it: *Yes*.

We filed for divorces.

Like a coward, I told Gil I was doing this because I planned to come clean with the IRS. I'd long wanted to pay the years of back taxes we owed and avoid possible prosecution. Gil had always refused to do it, and he did so again now, as I'd known he would. I argued that it would be easier for me if we weren't married. There was truth in that, but obviously, it was not the story. Gil went along. He asked no questions; I've never known why. Maybe he had his own reasons for welcoming a divorce. Or maybe, in spite of his jealousy, he thought nothing would change. Maybe, in spite of his own infidelities, he could not conceive of mine.

And then a friend in whom Vinnie had confided the affair told Vinnie's wife, and she told Gil.

He moved out, came back two days later, and moved out again. This pattern repeated, while his clothes never left the closet. He said we were still married—he said we'd always be married, that he would never allow me to leave him. He was often drunk, or high, which stoked his rage. I did not defend myself, certain it would only make everything worse, but it was also true I had betrayed him. It was during this period that he told me he'd once killed a man.

Whenever he was home, I spoke to him as little as possible. I tried not to look at him, because it set him off, but not looking at him also provoked him. I enrolled Amy in preschool, and took a full-time job. Vinnie wanted me to get out, but I hoped this season of Gil moving in and out would pass and that I'd be able to remain in our reasonably priced apartment. It was the girls' home. "Possession is nine-tenths, change the locks," my attorney told me. Gil, I knew, would just break a window. The attorney said, "He's blowing off steam. Wait him out. Whatever you do, don't leave the apartment. As long as you stay there, it's yours."

Late one night, with Gil camped out in our bed and snoring

drunkenly, I got on the phone to Vinnie. He was in Florida, visiting his parents; his father was ill. I said I wished he was with me. He said I should move down to LA.

While I quietly talked, saying God knows what else, a voice emerged from nowhere. "Go ahead," Gil crooned. "Try it, Kerry."

He lay flat on his back on the living room floor, not five feet away, the lower half of his body hidden in the hallway. I hung up the phone without saying goodbye; it was terrible, but my every nerve screamed and I could do nothing else. I went immediately to Gil. It was as if a monster had drawn me against all reason into his lair. I stood over him, fighting the urge to get down on the floor.

"What to do, what to do," Gil hummed.

I asked—I couldn't help it: "What are you thinking?"

"Snakes and filth, baby. Snakes and filth."

My ears buzzed, my teeth chattered.

"You don't want to know," he said. "But I'm telling you. You're going to."

IT WAS AN eight-hour drive south to Lakeshore Gardens, the mobile home park in Carlsbad, California, where Mom had retired. The girls slept through it all.

At the front gate I leaned out the window and punched in the security code. I cruised past the park's clubhouse where Mom played bridge twice a week, and the boomerang-shaped swimming pool, careful to keep to the posted speed limit of nine and three-quarters miles per hour. Coastal fog veiled palm trees and the communal lawns that ran between homes and behind them. Near the park's southern edge, I turned onto Mom's street. My stomach flipped at the sight of her yellow-and-white triple-wide.

I parked in the driveway and cut the engine. It ticked like a bomb. I reached into the rear seat and woke up the girls. By the time we were out of the car, Mom was at her back door. We'd left in the middle of the night—I didn't tell her we were coming. She hid her surprise behind kisses and hugs, a hustle to get the girls inside, where coffee was brewing and the day's earliest cigarettes had already burnt down to their filters in her abalone-shell ashtray. Mom and I set the girls up at the table with bowls of cornflakes. Erin concentrated on eating, while Amy chattered and stirred her cereal into soup. I sat across from Mom, hands wrapped around a hot mug. She barely looked at me. She asked no questions. She was biding her time.

WE PACKED HER Volvo with folding chairs, with sweatshirts and towels and a cooler filled with sandwiches and supermarket soda. Mom retrieved plastic buckets and scoops from her storage shed, along with a mayonnaise jar for collecting shells. The beach was only three blocks away, but the air felt noticeably cooler there. Few people were out, only an older couple walking along the shore and a cluster of bikinied teenagers determined, despite the weather, to tan.

Mom sat in a beach chair in her windbreaker and a pink baseball cap, working the *LA Times* crossword puzzle. In between supervising the girls in the shallows, I vegetated alongside her, hypnotized by the frothing whitecaps. Shadows of seagulls passed overhead. The girls played tag with the waves and shrieked at sand crabs. The three of us built a castle. We gave it turrets, round crenelated towers, a keep.

Mom set down her newspaper and pen. "What happened, Kerry?" she asked. "I thought you were happy."

My throat constricted. I'd lied about my marriage for so long.

Mom hefted her carryall into her lap, dug through Lifesavers and bottles of Tylenol, pencils, postcards, and old church bulletins. She pulled out her Benson & Hedges, a lighter, and a packet of Kleenex.

She passed me the tissues, then tipped a smoke from the pack. She cupped a shaking hand against the wind and lit up.

I didn't want my mother's pity, and I was wary of help. I knew she loved me, but I also knew I was a failure in her eyes. Now the price of my pride had come due. I confessed to falling in love with someone else, and to filing for a divorce. I expected accusations of weakness and the usual bemoaning of my lack of common sense. I preferred that her disappointment shape itself around my immorality. Instead she asked, "Is it the drinking?"

I swallowed hard. "Among other things."

Mom lowered her voice. "Does he hit you?"

"I don't love him."

"Oh, grow up, Kerry."

When I was small, my idea of a grown-up had been a woman in a dress wearing stockings and heels. Mom let me rummage in her closet sometimes, let me play dress-up and put on her makeup. Carrying a handheld mirror, I'd wobble around in absurdly high heels, alternately admiring my red-lipsticked mouth and tilting the mirror so I could see the ceiling and pretend to walk on the beams.

"Who's the man?" she asked.

"Vinnie," I said.

"I see." The words were freighted. My mother had met Vinnie. She knew he was a friend. But she didn't *know* him. "Out of the frying pan," she sighed.

"I love him," I said.

"Ugh," she said. "Love."

EVERY EVENING, AFTER we put the girls to bed, Mom and I sat at the countertop that divided the kitchen from her den, drinking wine from jelly glasses and watching some comforting program on TV. On the fifth night, while Sam and Woody vied for Rebecca's favors on *Cheers*, the telephone rang. I knew it was Gil; I knew it like I knew my own name.

Mom didn't answer—she also knew.

Brrinng brrinng.

I picked up with a strangled "Hello."

"There you are," Gil said cheerfully. "I was wondering." When I failed to respond, he said, "Thought you might be in LA—You been in LA?"

"No," I managed.

"Your little friend's disappeared." He meant, of course, Vinnie. "But I'm sure you know that. Is he there with you?"

"No."

"You sure?"

"I don't want to talk about this now, Gil."

He cleared his throat. "Put Dorothy on. She needs to know what a slut her daughter is." I might have laughed at this, if I wasn't so scared. What did he think? That Mom would choose him over me? But, "Never mind," he said, changing tack. "Put the girls on. I want to talk to them."

"It's late, Gil. They're asleep. We spent all day at the beach. They were really tired. They—" I stopped this overexplaining.

"You put sunscreen on 'em?"

"Yes," I said. Then, "Goddamn it."

I heard sounds of him moving around, something dropped to the floor.

"I wanna call a truce, Kerry. Come home. Please." His voice

cracked on the word. And doubt came flooding in. He said plaintively, "You have to come home."

I could not stay at Mom's. Gil and I had unfinished business. I had a job I couldn't afford to lose, and I didn't want Erin to miss her final week of first grade.

"You can't be there," I said. "Will you be there?"

After a long silence he said, "Not if you don't want me to be."

THE KEY IN the lock. The front door opening. I carried one child, heavy with sleep; the other child clung to me. We stepped into the dark, a hollow silence that felt predatory. Faint smell of fire. I tensed from head to toe and waited for my eyes to adjust. Slowly, outlines of our furniture emerged: the piano, the couch, the coffee table.

"Sweetheart," I said softly to Erin. "Can you turn the lamp on?"

She did, and the living room came glowing to life.

"Daddy?" she said.

No answer. Gil had kept his word. "Daddy's not here," I said.

I led her into the bedroom and lowered Amy onto the bed. Erin climbed up. They both still had on their playclothes, but fuck it. I tucked them in. If Gil could've seen, I would have heard about it.

In the living room I knelt by the fireplace and stuck a hand over the ashes. Bits of unburned paper were mixed in, nothing I could identify. Did they still give off heat? I thought so, but it might've been my imagination.

I sat back on my heels.

A car pulled into the building's parking lot, its headlights shining in through cracks in our window blinds. An engine shut off and the headlights went out. A car door slammed. It was three in the morning—was it Gil? Had he been watching? I couldn't know without checking, but I was frozen in place. The building's front door opened, and I heard footsteps in the entry, then the sound of someone climbing the stairs. It was only a neighbor coming in late.

I scrambled to my feet and looked all around. The piano, the couch, the coffee table, everything as it should be. My eye settled on the basket we filled with the girls' toys. Behind it, a row of framed photographs hung on the wall. Something was off there.

I moved closer.

The first photo was one I'd always loved of Gil and Mom, taken at the reception on our wedding day. Gil had an arm thrown companionably around Mom's shoulder; he was looking at her and laughing. She seemed caught off guard by his affection, a genuine smile on her face.

The next frame, however, was empty. The strangeness of this made me queasy. I ran a finger tentatively over the glass. For the life of me, I couldn't remember what had been there.

The next picture was of the girls flying a kite in Golden Gate Park. They looked so small under that sky. Then came another from the wedding, Gil and I alone on the church steps. Something was wrong here as well. *Oh.* Gil was headless.

What had he done?

I ran to the kitchen, crouched before a low cabinet, and threw open its door. We kept piles of random paperwork here, paid utility bills and warranties, my night-class term papers and a few short stories I'd written, and the girls' growing childhood ephemera. Mine, too: a robot novel I wrote at age nine, an assigned autobiography from eighth grade. The girls' stuff all seemed to be intact. Mine, however, was missing. I opened the next cabinet, looking for our family photographs, and was relieved to see all the albums neatly stacked. I removed a shoebox that held more recent snapshots. Most were of our daughters: sleeping, bathing, eating, playing. I dumped the contents onto the floor and sifted through, unable to tell if anything was missing. I came upon a shot of Gil and me mutilated in the same way as the wedding photo in the living room, his head cleanly scissored out. Eyeing the stacked albums with dread, I pulled out our wedding book. Slowly I turned its pages. He'd cut his head out of several photos. If he'd sliced me away, it would've made a horrible kind of sense, but this? It was so disturbing.

Here now was the picture of Vinnie and me at the reception, standing near the dance floor. My image was unharmed, but Gil had repeatedly stabbed something into Vinnie's neck. His wrath was palpable. A shiver of fear for Vinnie's safety ran through me.

The missing print in the living room, I suddenly remembered, was of me as a child.

That smell of fire. Those bits of paper.

Had he—? No. He wouldn't.

I slid out my baby album and opened it up. Every photo was gone.

Mom's old albums were next. She'd given them to me for safekeeping after selling the house in LA. I flipped through them. My arms grew heavy, my fingers numb. All those ancient black-and-white photos with scalloped edges and sepia stains—gone. Portraits of my grandparents that I knew so well, snapshots of aunts and uncles and cousins, everyone gathered at backyard barbecues with drinks in their hands and smiling faces—gone. Shots of Daddy in knickers, in his Air Force uniform. Mom in a saggy-bottomed woolen swimsuit, lined up with her siblings on the sand at Rockaway. All gone. As a kid I'd spent hours with these images, with these people, constructing for myself a surrogate ancestry. Gil had destroyed everything.

One last item remained in the cabinet. My strongbox.

My pulse quickened. *No, no, no, no.*

I pulled the box out, set it in my lap, and entered the combination, 6–5–3, Gil's height and mine. The lock tumbled. I removed birth certificates, bank books and rental agreements, the pink slips for our cars. At bottom sat a brown letter-sized envelope. Inside it I'd kept a love letter from 1973 and the Polaroid photograph of my son. I opened the flap. The envelope was empty.

I doubled over, wailing. Then clapped a hand to my mouth. *Don't wake the girls. Don't scare them.* Tears ran down my cheeks. They dripped from my fingers and chin. Gil had custom-designed this punishment, this erasure, laying waste to my childhood artifacts, my stabs at writing, my family's history. Out of sheer malevolence he'd burned the only photograph I had of my son.

I struggled to my feet—I had to get on my feet. My knees wobbled, and I felt like I might fall, but I didn't fall. I couldn't, because of the girls.

I hurried now to the bedroom, where they lay on their sides, backs touching. Oh, the curve of Erin's cheek. Amy's toddler snores. My daughters were right here. I scooted Amy over and slid in. I needed sleep—everything would look different after sleep. In the morning I'd call Vinnie and we'd decide together what to do next.

I awoke two hours later, a rosy sunrise creeping through the bedroom window. Automatically, I headed to the kitchen. The cabinet's contents still littered the floor, so I started a pot of coffee, and I put everything back. I poured a cup and sat. Another day. My mind emptied. When I heard the girls stirring, I got up and filled a pot of water for oatmeal.

A bullet sat dead center between the stove's burners. It looked like the world's tiniest missile.

It was a message from Gil. A promise. A plan.

7

The Giant Dipper

I called Vinnie at his parents' house in Florida and told him about the photographs: Gil cutting his own head off, Gil stabbing Vinnie in the neck, the ashes in the fireplace. I told him about the bullet. I knew I sounded incoherent, my words slurry, and tumbling.

"Hang up right now, Kerry," he said. "I want you to call the police."

"I *can't.*"

"Get out of the apartment then. Now. I'll call the airline and get a flight and meet you in LA."

Vinnie didn't understand how this would make everything worse. He didn't have years of experience with how Gil reacted when challenged, how he operated when he felt he'd been wronged.

But I had a plan.

When I'd filed for divorce, my attorney told me I could move the girls ninety miles away from Gil without having to petition the court. On a map of California it looked like nothing, a matter of scale, but by the clock, from our apartment in Kentfield it would take nearly two hours. If I did this, Gil could still see his daughters, but he'd be forced to think twice about showing up unannounced.

I loaded our suitcases back into the car, threw more clothes into grocery sacks, and stuffed them on top with toys and books, my strongbox, and the shoebox of photographs, all this frantic activity driven by angst that Gil would return. I woke the girls, handed them toaster waffles, and led them out to the car. They protested. They didn't understand. They shouldn't have had to.

I drove us south over the Golden Gate Bridge, through the western part of the city and onto Highway 1, which snaked along the coast. The farther we got from the apartment, the calmer I felt. At the ninety-mile mark, we entered Santa Cruz on West Cliff Drive. I'd been through the town many times but had never stopped. Large houses lined one side of the street; on the other a footpath weaved through banks of purple ice plant. From up on the cliff, the Pacific Ocean looked like a spill of blue paint. We rounded a curve into a sudden aerial view of the boardwalk. Erin excitedly picked out the rollercoaster and a Ferris wheel. Amy clapped her hands. My head spun. *What had I done?*

Downtown, I stopped at a phone booth to call Vinnie's apartment, but it was too soon for him to be home. I called work and told my boss how sorry I was to leave them in the lurch, but I had to quit. At a thrift store, I bought sheets and blankets for an apartment we didn't yet have. This was what you did. One foot in front of the other. I picked up a local newspaper at a stand, and while the girls ate ice-cream cones—a bribe, a reward—I perused the classifieds, circling rentals. By mid-afternoon I'd signed a one-year lease on the top half of a duplex in the Seabright neighborhood; it sat around the corner from a Chinese restaurant, a bakery, a bar, and a convenience store that rented videos. The duplex was dilapidated but fenced. The entrance to the upstairs apartment was hidden behind a locked gate. A plum tree heavy with fruit grew in the yard, and windows wrapped all around, and the small balcony offered a slivered view of the sea. It felt like a place to begin again.

By nighttime I'd reached Vinnie. He'd be on his way north tomorrow early. The girls and I curled up on the living-room floor to the sounds of barking seals and muted screams coming from the boardwalk. The air smelled of salt. Through the curtainless windows, the night was glowing with moonlight, gauzy with fog.

THE GIRLS HAD known Vinnie since they were born and were surprisingly unsurprised when he turned up, his truck loaded with twin mattresses, a television and VCR, a loveseat, a couple of chairs, dishes, and some basic cookware. We made another trip to the thrift store to fill in the blanks. Vinnie said that he wanted to see Gil, to discuss the bullet on the stove and to tell him he had to leave me alone. But this so visibly panicked me he agreed for the time being to lay low. Maybe, we reasoned, now that I'd finally left, it would all blow over. We took the girls out to dinner at the Chinese restaurant, then the four of us walked along train tracks that crossed a bridge spanning the San Lorenzo River. Below lay the boardwalk.

The cavernous arcade, once a casino, clanged with gaming. There was Skee-Ball, pinball, air hockey, Indy 500 and space-travel video games. It was Vegas for kids. We played a few rounds before wandering out to the midway, crowded with coeds in bikinis, surfer dudes, packs of tweens, and entire families. The girls asked to go on the bumper cars. Vinnie paired up with Amy. We all made a point of seeking each other out and *ramming* our cars. The Giant Dipper looked tempting, but Amy was too young and Erin too scared— the ride had been designed as "combination earthquake, balloon ascension, and aeroplane drop." Still, we enjoyed tracking the terrified riders. We got in line for Logger's Revenge, a more modest water coaster, and emerged laughing and elated and soaked to the bone. I breathed in the perfume of suntan lotion, the burnt-sugar smell of waffle cones. Vinnie bought the girls hot dogs and cotton candy—who could say no? When the sun set, we joined a mob on the sand for a free concert of faded rock-and-rollers and old-time R&B, Santa Cruz's "Friday Night Bands on the Beach." I felt lucky in our random selection of a new home.

For a week, we vacationed.

We took the girls up into the forested hills east of town, to the Mystery Spot, a purported gravitational anomaly where balls rolled uphill, and where I towered over Vinnie, who was a foot taller than me. We took them to Capitola, a pastel wedge of a burgh a few miles south of Santa Cruz, where the surf was extra gentle. We swam and walked the shore.

Watching the girls play in the waves, Vinnie and I talked about our childhoods.

He told me how, as a youngster in Long Island, New York, he'd lived summers at the neighborhood pool, spending all day in the water, more fish than human; and on weekends, his Italian family would trek to the beach, hauling across the hot sand coolers, totes filled with changes of clothes, blankets, beach chairs, towels, umbrellas. Vinnie would bodysurf the entire day, emerging shivering and blue-lipped only to eat.

His favorite outing had been riding the subway with his grandpa out to Coney Island. They wore T-shirts and swim trunks and carried nothing but a towel slung over one shoulder. They bought food when they arrived—Nathan's hot dogs with lots of mustard and pickle relish. Oh, the liberty! Vinnie's grandpa had a workshop in the basement of his Brooklyn home, and he'd taught Vinnie how to hammer nails and saw wood, how to put things together, how to assess them. Take an armoire, or a kitchen appliance, Vinnie said. Most people see these items as a mysterious whole, but inside, it's all been slotted into an exact place, and everything interacts with everything else. Once you understand how something is built and functions, the whole is no longer a mystery. Learning this from his grandpa made Vinnie feel he could make or fix anything.

When he was nine, he used to daydream about sleeping with a girl. He'd had no one specific in mind. He didn't yet know about sex; it was a more innocent time. He couldn't even conceive of touching. But the idea of lying side by side under the covers thrilled him.

In turn, I told him about Frannie, the daughter of Daddy's best friend. The family lived in La Cañada, near Pasadena, in the kind of neighborhood I'd longed for, with lawns and swimming pools, flat streets where you could ride a bike, and in the summer, gangs of kids that ran around outside from after breakfast until the moms, with dinner on the table, screamed them home again. Whenever we visited La Cañada, Frannie, who was three years older than me, found herself stuck with a cringeworthy junior associate. Daddy and Uncle Frank would be out playing golf for most of the day, while Mom and Aunt Sally set themselves up at the dining room table and played a three-deck card game called Samba. Through the wall Frannie and I heard girlish laughter and periodic accusations of cheating. *Dorothy, you dirty dog!* The two of us dorked around with Frannie's Barbies—I always had to be Ken—and when we ran out of wardrobe changes and plot, we switched to Concentration. We played with three decks, just like our moms, spreading them all over the floor. When Frannie grew bored, she'd sink into a trance and call up Francessina. Francessina, who looked exactly like my beloved cousin, was a dark creature, greedy and sadistic and manipulative, with a sinister glamour I admired. She lived in an alternate world called Marineland. There, kids could be whoever they wanted, say and do whatever they wanted, and what they wanted most was to be bad. I knew about bad. Lying, for instance was bad. Stealing dimes from Mom's purse was bad. Removing my pajama bottoms under the covers and touching my body as if it belonged to someone else was very bad.

Ah, so this was why I'd told Vinnie this story—I wished I'd been the girl he dreamed of sleeping beside.

Francessina would proclaim, *God you're ugly,* and I'd nod at her wise cruelty, then beg her to show me how to become Kerrisina. But Frannie knew an advantage when she had one and would not let me transform.

For all our attraction to each other, and for all the years we'd already been friends, the telling of these stories—and the listening to them—led Vinnie and I into greater intimacy.

I lifted a fistful of sand, let it trickle through my fingers. And told him then about my teenage pregnancy, about hiding in San Clemente and at St. Anne's. I told him about giving away my baby, and how Gil had burned the only photograph I had of my son.

Vinnie cupped my cheek in his hand.

I loved everything about him. His kind eyes, his long feet, the way one shoulder rode higher than the other and on that side wore his shirts thin. I loved the smell of him, clean sweat and furniture oil. I loved the sound of his voice, which soothed like the sea. I loved his colorful, rational self, no mental gymnastics necessary. Freedom from fear was exhilarating. For the first time in forever, I didn't doubt reality. For the first time in forever, normal might mean happy.

It didn't last, of course.

Vinnie had work waiting in LA and had to return. He'd be back as soon as he could.

Meanwhile, there was Gil.

ON THE PHONE I told him I'd left him for good, that we'd moved to Santa Cruz permanently. When he said I couldn't do that, I said, "I can. And I have." Because of the bullet he'd left on the stove, I refused to give him our phone number or address. How unrecognizably firm I sounded. Gil probably had a right to this information, but I needed time and a little more peace. I waited for him to ask to speak to the girls. Instead, he insisted he had to see me. He proposed meeting halfway, just the two of us. There was a Chart House restaurant on Highway 1, right on the water, south of Moss Landing.

"Tomorrow, Kerry?"

That we used to eat at the Chart House in Sausalito on special occasions seemed cause for worry. I didn't want to meet him now, or like this. Vinnie didn't want me meeting Gil under any circumstance. But the issue of custody hung over me. Gil was Erin and Amy's father. I couldn't keep him from his children.

"C'mon," he said. "We can have lunch. I'll buy."

WHEN I TURNED into the Chart House parking lot, mine was the only car. The restaurant, all wooden shingles and smoky glass angled to mimic the waves, looked abandoned, a layer of trash blown along the side of the building. It must have gone out of business. Did Gil know? I sat in the car, thinking about what that might mean. If he failed to show, it would not be the worst thing.

After a while, I got out and walked toward the edge of the cliff. It was a windy day, the ocean roiling. I expected a dramatic drop down to the sand, but the perception of height was an illusion. Four feet below, a harmless chop rolled. A short jump and I could've stuck my feet in.

I turned at the crunch of wheels on gravel. It was Gil in a red sports car I'd never seen. The last I knew, he'd just leased a brand-new Hyundai, with nothing down and zero percent interest—I'd never understood how he did it. He executed a quick three-point turn and backed the car up until our vehicles sat tail to tail. There was little traffic on Highway 1; we were alone here. Dread settled over me.

Gil shut off his engine. He opened the door and unfolded from the low seat like a praying mantis. He leaned against the fender, as if catching his breath, and then walked slowly toward me. I walked slowly toward him. The closer I got, the worse he looked. His nose was swollen. Scabs striped his left cheek. He wore a brace on one wrist. Something—or someone—had blackened his eye.

"Good God, what happened?" I asked.

"Relax," he said. "I'm fine. Looks a lot worse than it is."

"What *happened*? Did you get in a brawl?"

"I crashed the Hyundai last night. In the city. Wrecked it so bad I walked away. Had to get the hell out of there before they showed up with the breathalyzer."

"Whose car is this?" I asked.

"Belongs to Bernard." He was one of Gil's art-sales buddies, a man I'd heard of but never met.

"They'll come after you," I said.

"First they have to find me." He winked. It looked like it hurt. "Crashing was *fun*, Kerry. Wheee!"

Was he covering up embarrassment? Or admitting he found damage arousing? And why didn't he wait until he was healed to meet? He must've wanted me to see. He must've been counting on sympathy.

He tipped his chin at the Chart House. "Guess we're not having lunch."

We could've gone elsewhere, but I didn't suggest it and neither did he. This felt like progress. I breathed a little easier.

He walked back to the sports car and opened the hatch. "I've got stuff for you." He looked at me over a shoulder. "Stop acting like a scared rabbit. Come here, I ain't gonna bite. You have to open your trunk."

I scooted into the space between our two cars while fumbling in my bag for the key. I unlocked the trunk. Gil moved a few things into it before saying, "Give me a hand." We transferred a mish-mash of items, mostly kitchenware: a coffee-maker, our old crockpot, the blender. The girls and I could use it all, but I didn't feel like saying thank you. My hair lifted in the wind. Gil's shirttail flapped. An unexpected whiff of Aqua Net sent me reeling. This was the closest I'd been to him physically in weeks, and the urge to get away was overwhelming.

"Why did you go?" he asked suddenly.

"Are you kidding me? You know."

"Say it."

"You left a bullet for me."

"No. Vinnie's the reason."

"He is." I set down a box filled with utensils. "But he's not the only reason. You know that. You *know*."

"I want you to take me seriously."

"We're not married anymore, Gil. I'm not your—Why'd you cut your head out of the photos?"

A smile transformed his injured face. "I only did that to the ones of you and me."

"But why?"

"I was *depriving* you of me. Don't you get it? I'm out of your life."

This was a warped way of seeing things, but at least he

understood we were through. A lump came up in my throat. "You burned the photograph of my son!"

"Yeah." The light in his eyes died. "I'm sorry about that. I am. But I'm turning over a new leaf. Starting now. I could've died in that wreck . . . so, no more drinking." He'd never said this before— it gave me hope. He scrubbed his face with his palm. "From here on out, I ain't gonna bother you. You deserve a life. I know that. I'm gonna respect your privacy. But you have to let me see the girls when I want to, you have to tell me where they live, you have to let me talk to them on the phone. I need to be able to call them. I need the number. Please."

At this mention of our daughters, I was brimming.

A demonstration of trust here might be a way to make things better between us. I allowed in another wisp of hope, desperate for Gil to see reason, but also for him to be okay. I didn't want to fight about every last fucking thing.

We stood in the tight space between the cars. I looked up at him. He looked down at me.

I gave him what he sought. He wrote nothing down—he didn't need to. And I remembered something he used to say: *I was an elephant before I got into sales.*

He leaned closer. "You think you can get rid of me? You can't. And you never will. I'll haunt you in your dreams."

I went lightheaded. *No, no, no, no.*

He stepped closer. I felt trapped but didn't dare show it.

"You're gonna do what I want, Kerry," he said. "You're gonna stop seeing Vinnie. Or I'll take the children away."

When Gil and Rita were divorcing, he'd sued her for custody, and they'd battled for more than a year. At a hearing, his attorney had called her mother and brother to the stand to grill them about Rita's drinking. When in the end Gil didn't prevail, he was incensed. *They lied*, he said. *And I should've known, blood being thicker than water.*

The way he'd been living, I didn't see how he could win custody of Erin and Amy either. But who knew?

He gestured at the back of the sports car. "I could throw you in there. Drive you out to the desert and bury you in a place no one will ever find." He slammed shut the hatch. "Maybe next time."

After all these years, had I learned nothing? Now he knew where we were.

8

White of the Eye

found a job at a semiconductor firm in Scotts Valley, and enrolled the girls in school. Fall inched into winter. I assumed Gil would drive down often to visit the girls, but he made the trip sporadically, calling when he was nearly on our doorstep. I refused to let him into the duplex or to take Erin and Amy on his own. We met downtown, at a bookstore, or a park. It was a disaster every time.

Initially he'd focus on his daughters, but soon he'd shift attention to me. Oozing contempt, he denigrated my work ethic, my cooking, my mothering: I was a spike in hard ground he relished hammering. He'd also failed to turn over that supposed leaf. He snuck sips from a flask and ducked into alleys to snort crank; he smelled like chemicals burning. I told Gil he needed help, and he said, as he always had, "I can quit anytime." And then he said, "You don't do what I want, Kerry, you're gonna be sorry."

What he wanted never changed: I had to give up Vinnie.

Vinnie and I held off on him moving in. He still wanted to meet up with Gil, to resolve things, but I was so viscerally alarmed by the idea, my weeping so fervid, he let it go. Call the lawyer, he suggested. Which I did. But nothing could be done without police reports and a hearing, and I knew that that would make Gil worse.

Gil phoned me at all hours. If I answered, he was abusive. If I hung up, he left messages. *Hey cunt, why won't you get back to me? . . . Where are you? Are you there? It's over. Sayonara. . . . Have a miserable fucking holiday, eighty-nine is going to be a shit year.* Vinnie and I talked evenings, after the girls went to bed. If Gil called then and the line was busy, he immediately called Vinnie. If Vinnie's line was busy . . . The thing was: all of Gil's assumptions were correct.

Finally, I contacted the police. I explained what life was like for us, the nature of Gil's threats, and how I lived with constant fear. They advised a restraining order, which I'd already decided was impossible. Once served, he'd be on my doorstep. If they arrested and then later released him, he'd come after me hard. Desperate, I had a second phone line installed for Vinnie's calls. That provided some relief but didn't help with the constant ringing. All I could do was unplug the phone.

If too many days passed with no answer, Gil got in the car and headed to Santa Cruz.

Weeks went by and nothing changed.

Vinnie, arriving in Santa Cruz after his long drive up from LA, would park somewhere with a view of my rear balcony. If the coast was clear, I'd tie a handkerchief to the railing. If not, he'd check into a motel, waiting until I came to get him.

Living like this was insane.

Meanwhile, Vinnie's divorce was finalized. Mine, however, had stalled. Gil wouldn't hire an attorney nor apply for legal aid. His friend Bernard had taken over the lease on our apartment, and I was pretty sure Gil was living there, but process servers had no luck finding him. The office mailed Gil papers, which he forwarded to me with a scrawled message, *Fuck you, Kerry!*

Just after New Year's, someone threw rotten meat into the yard. Then someone superglued the lock to the gate. Someone slashed my tires in a drugstore parking lot. I couldn't prove it, but I knew it was Gil stalking me. Being forever on edge was painful. My head throbbed, my chest ached. I had trouble sleeping. And the worse I felt, the less clear my thinking.

One morning, after arriving at work, the front desk paged me to the lobby, where Gil was waiting. He rained down accusations while I twisted my hands, longing to plug my ears. The receptionist, glimpsed over Gil's shoulder, looked concerned. Gil's voice rose.

"They should know what kind of person you are! A cheat and a liar."

Afraid of losing my job, I walked straight out through the front doors. Gil, behind me, called my name. I scurried around the side of the building and sprinted for my car. I'd almost made it when he grabbed me, and spun me to face him, and gripped my upper arms. The pine groves that climbed the hill behind the parking lot were steeped in shade. The air felt warm, much drier than near the beach. Traffic rumbled on nearby Highway 17. My limbs loosened. I felt myself dissociating.

"I sold your fucking piano," Gil said. "*Twice*. Once to a couple, then to some teacher. I had it delivered then got outta Dodge." I moaned and he laughed. "Bernard's good at playing dumb."

I flashed back years, to the cops at our doorstep in LA, me denying I'd ever heard of Gil.

"Forty thousand dollars, baby," he said. "Should I throw you a bone? A couple of bucks to help out? . . . I've been doing collections. A woman bought a painting from Bernard but never paid." He tightened his hold. "I broke into her apartment. Went in through a bedroom window while she was asleep. Stuck a gun in her face."

I trembled—was it the gun he'd pointed at me?

"That woke her up, Kerry. And guess what? She *paid*. And I'll tell you this, it was *invigorating*. Got my blood up."

"You're a sick man."

"For fuck's sake, I didn't *hurt* her." As if genuinely curious, he asked, "You scared of me?"

Admit I was and it would excite him. Say I wasn't and who knew. I craned my neck, trying to see the building's rear entry. Where the hell was security?

"No one's coming to save you," Gil said.

He took my head in his hands, turned it, and stared into my eyes. I thought he meant to kiss me. His hands tightened over my ears and he threw his head forward. A sharp crack to the top of my brow, then release. I crumpled but didn't fall. When I looked up, he was gone.

A WEEK LATER, Gil made an appointment with my attorney. He wanted to demonstrate, live and in person, that his intentions were pure, that he meant me no harm. I would be charged for this meeting.

Afterward, the attorney phoned. "That's a nice guy," he said. "He doesn't care about you or your love life. He's concerned about his children."

"Fucking hell. I'm the *mother* of his children."

"Yes, but you moved them away."

"You told me I could!"

The attorney went quiet.

"If he really cared about the girls," I said, "he wouldn't make death threats. He wouldn't act like a crazed stalker. He *head-butted* me."

"Did you go to Urgent Care?" the attorney asked.

He knew I did not.

"Did you take pictures?"

"The bruise is mostly buried in my hairline. You can barely see it."

"So it wasn't that bad."

"It was bad. I saw stars."

"Well," the attorney said, "divorce is messy. But he can't keep it up forever, he's got his own life. Honestly, he seemed okay. I think he's bluffing."

My heart sank. There would be no real help here. Was it the old boys' club at work? Or had Gil simply charmed him? Whatever anyone heard in advance about Gil never seemed to matter, because he was a salesman first and always, and he knew how to win people over.

IN FEBRUARY BOTH girls came down with chicken pox, itchy, fluid-filled sores that covered their faces, torsos, and legs before spreading to the insides of their mouths and ears. They radiated misery and scratched until they bled. I persuaded Gil to stay away while I took time off from work, but when the virus persisted, Vinnie drove up to care for them. He dabbed calamine lotion onto their lesions. He made them pasta. He played Wheel of Fortune with Erin, she taking the part of Pat Sajak, while he did the announcer's voice plus all of the guests. He rigged a sheet of cardboard as a sled, then sat at the bottom of the staircase. The girls rode down, squealing.

They recovered and went back to school, but at some point Erin must have said something to Gil, because the next time he called, she turned to me and held out the phone.

"Daddy wants you."

I took the receiver. "What."

He launched in. "Maybe you don't care about yourself, Kerry, but what if I go after your dopey boyfriend? Will that get your attention?"

He began to leave messages on Vinnie's answering machine.

He drove down to LA and slashed Vinnie's tires, which convinced me he'd been the one who had slashed mine weeks ago. He edged under Vinnie's front door a newspaper article about a man who'd murdered his child's molester but did no jail time.

One weekend, when the girls and I visited Vinnie on the way back from Mom's, we discovered sticks of dynamite lying sideways on the windshield wipers of his truck. They'd been rubber-banded together, fuses twined like a twist tie on a bag of bread and stuck into the end of a cigar with a half-inch of ash. It seemed likely that Gil had lit the fuse and run, and the fuse died before detonating. Vinnie's truck was parked just underneath the apartment. Did Gil know that the girls were upstairs? If the dynamite had gone off . . . I couldn't imagine it.

Vinnie called the West Hollywood Sheriff's Department, and two deputies dropped by for a look. "That's enough to blow up the building," they said, sounding impressed.

"Yes, and I know who did it," Vinnie said.

"Who would that be?"

"Did you look at the file? I've reported his threats before—my girlfriend's ex-husband calls all the time to say he's coming to kill me."

I'd listened to the messages: nine a.m., *I'm on my way*; two in the afternoon, *Hey scumbag, get ready;* four o'clock, *You'll never see me coming.* Sometimes Vinnie sat up all night, watching his front door.

"Sounds like big talk," said one of the deputies. "You need to contact us when he's inside."

Vinnie gestured at the dynamite. "He was right here."

"Could be you, though."

"What?" Vinnie was incredulous. "You think I put explosives on my own truck? Come on."

"The problem is, we can't prove it was him."

This is a crime scene, I wanted to scream. Couldn't they at least take fingerprints?

"Will you talk to him?" Vinnie asked.

Brightening, they said they would, but when they learned that Gil lived in Northern California, they changed their tune. They didn't have jurisdiction there. And we were back to square one.

THE NEXT TIME Gil called, Vinnie answered, and they agreed to meet. "We can work through our differences, man to man," Gil said. Vinnie thought this sounded promising, but to me it felt ominous. I tried to dissuade him, but he said, "It'll be good, Kerry. We're meeting in public, at Hamburger Hamlet, the one on the Strip. It's been a year, and we're all still stuck. Maybe if he says whatever he has to to my face . . ." Just in case, he'd stick a micro recorder in a pocket and get Gil on tape.

When he arrived at the restaurant, Gil was seated, the waiter laughing at something he'd said. Vinnie, on the way to the table, hit RECORD. This tape would turn out to be useless, not one word legible. Vinnie took a seat, the waiter handed them menus, they placed their orders. Food came and they began to eat. They were halfway through the meal before either one spoke.

Gil, eyeing Vinnie, squinted appraisingly. "You look like shit."

This was true. Vinnie had lost forty pounds he couldn't spare.

"Maybe you got AIDS?"

"No," Vinnie said. But he'd detected in Gil's tone a note of sympathy, a ghost of his former self, with its New York–style camaraderie. It reminded him, painfully, how they used to be friends. "Why don't we—"

"You hear about Noriega?" Gil interrupted.

"Who?" Vinnie said, baffled.

"Manuel Noriega. Panama."

"Oh. Yeah. Wasn't he indicted on drug trafficking? He'll do serious time."

"Gotta catch him first." Gil ate a french fry. "What about the Oscars?" he asked. "You used to want to be in the movies—who do you like for Best Actor? Dustin Hoffman? *Rain Man* was good. But there's also *Mississippi Burning*. Hackman! Always loved Popeye Doyle. How do you choose?"

Why was Gil talking about actors?

"Speaking of movies," Gil continued, "you see *White of the Eye*? Not exactly award-worthy, but it's still a great flick. It's got everything. Murder. Betrayal. *Hunting*. Cathy Moriarty reminds me of Kerry . . . Oh, hey!" He snapped his fingers. "Remember how I used to make calls for you in the phone room?"

Vinnie remembered. Gil sitting beside him, cold-calling on the WATS Line, running through a script he'd designed to overcome resistance.

"Vinnie the Guinea—you didn't have it, did you? But you were like a son to me."

The waiter came to collect their plates. "Dessert?"

"Nothing for me," Vinnie said.

"Yeah," Gil said. "We don't want any."

The waiter brushed crumbs from the tablecloth and departed.

Was that it? It was all so anticlimactic. Where to go next? Vinnie went with "You didn't treat Kerry right."

Gil leaned forward, his expression eager. "You're right. I didn't."

"Why?"

Gil shrugged. "Why'd you hurt *me*?"

"I didn't mean to fall in love."

"So you just wanted to fuck her?"

"No, I—"

"I get it, you *love* her. Isn't that right?"

"I do love her. And the girls. I love them. I'll take good care of them."

"Don't talk about my children! You have no fucking idea what it's like to have a family. There's a lot of responsibility. And you haven't exactly been responsible, have you? . . . Hey, you got my *special message*, right?"

"What? The dynamite?"

"Made an impression, I'll bet."

"This is ridiculous," Vinnie said. "Just leave us alone. Stop torturing Kerry."

"What you did to *your* wife was disgusting. Cheating! All she ever wanted was kids, you selfish prick. And now, because you *fell in love*, kids are hunky-dory?" Gil stood. "Looks like we're done." He rapped his knuckles on the table. "Walk me out to the car."

Maybe they should just slug it out, Vinnie thought. Maybe he should beat up Gil, if he could—or let Gil beat him.

"Don't be a pussy," Gil said. "Come outside with me."

But what would it solve?

"No," Vinnie said. "I'm good. You said it. We're done." Watching Gil leave, he thought sadly: Everything ventured, nothing gained.

WHEN THE SCHOOL year ended, I flew Erin down to Carlsbad to spend a week with Mom. Amy, who was too little and too wild, I kept home with me. Vinnie was having a busy month and remained in LA. It had been two weeks since his meeting with Gil, and we'd heard nothing. Maybe it worked, the Hamburger Hamlet meeting, in spite of how they'd left it. Maybe the worst was over, or on the way to being over. Erin's time with her grandmother passed as if she'd been returned to an easier, less complicated life, her days filled with clothes shopping and church and trips to the beach. Every night Mom made her a milkshake, which thrilled Erin—I'd never indulged her sweet tooth to that degree.

Her flight home to San Francisco International was due in late Saturday night. Amy and I would meet the plane. Vinnie was driving up to join us at the duplex early the next morning. Then we would all celebrate, together again, like a real family.

Mom called around the time I thought she was leaving for the airport.

"Gil's here," she said flatly. Hit by a vicious spike of adrenaline, I missed what she said next, hearing only "—on foot. He doesn't have a car, apparently."

"Jesus Christ. How'd he get there?"

"I don't know, Kerry. But he wants to escort Erin on the flight. He says he was visiting the kids" —his children with Rita, who were now teenagers— "but has to get home. Something about a deal. He thought he would, and I quote, 'kill two birds with one stone.'"

"Jesus Christ," I said again.

"He's got a ticket."

"Out of San Diego? That can't be. Did you ask to see it?"

"No."

"How did he know which flight to book?"

"I don't know!"

I heard voices in the background, Erin chattering. I heard Mom breathing.

"What do you want me to do?" she asked.

"You'll see them both onto the plane?" I said. "Stay at the gate until they're up in the air?"

"Of course I will." She sounded offended. "Of course."

I STOOD AT the gate, Amy a thirty-pound sack of potatoes in my arms, as the first passengers from San Diego disembarked. I composed my face into a mask of neutrality. People poured down the gateway, but no Erin, no Gil. A long pause, and another rush. The possibility they'd never gotten on the plane flashed through me. I pressed past other waiting families, trying for a better view. More passengers emerged. Now came a long stretch of nothing. A few stragglers trickled out, followed by the pilots and stewardesses, wheeling their bags. My stomach plummeted.

And then they appeared in the gateway, their faces familiar and loved, even Gil's. Amy squirmed excitedly—she'd spotted them, too. My jitters calmed. I was just an ordinary woman in an airport at midnight, meeting her dearly missed family.

When they were almost upon us, Gil fixed me with a glare. He exuded a hatred so pure it made my face burn.

I turned away. And here was my sweet seven-year-old, wearing what must've been a new outfit from Mom. Erin was all dark hair and long bangs, front teeth endearingly large though she wasn't smiling. I bent to hug her. Amy, wriggling, wanted down.

Gil held out his arms.

So I gave her to him—*I gave her to him.*

Gil buried his face in Amy's neck. He blew a raspberry, which made her giggle, then started off down the concourse. Erin and I followed, me carrying Erin's bag. Over Gil's shoulder, Amy stared back at us. Hair like pale feathers poked out from under her jacket's hood. Her bouncing face was like a blossom floating at the edge of a whirlpool, Gil's back both a wall that divided us and her sole support.

Let them get ahead a few steps. That was my thought. Time with the baby, even if fleeting, might do him good, her small self reminding him of his duty of care.

I needed to collect my emotions, anyway.

Another flight arrived and a clot of travelers surged down the concourse. Gil weaved through them. I picked up my pace, Erin trudging valiantly beside me. I squeezed her hand. "Did you have fun at Grandma's?"

She nodded.

"What did you like best?"

She looked up at me, her face full of fear.

No. Not fear. Despair.

I went down on one knee and hugged her again, hard. Her arms twined around my neck. I kissed the side of her head. Travelers streamed past us. Then Erin let go and I stood. The concourse had thinned, but I didn't see Gil. I didn't see Amy.

I wasn't worried. Not yet.

We walked on. I looked for a flight board and noted information for baggage claim. When we arrived at the carousel, I scanned the crush for Amy and Gil. Where were they? Maybe he'd made a pit stop on the way?

The first suitcases slid down the chute. A short wait, and there were more, some grabbed as they landed, others retrieved farther along.

Still no Amy and Gil.

I saw his bag, recognized it as one of two blue leather suitcases we'd bought in LA years ago. I pushed through, yanked the suitcase off the belt and moved both it and my daughter out of the way. We found an open spot near a pillar. Here we would wait.

Time passed.

Baggage from a different flight came in three carousels down. Maybe we were in the wrong spot? Was Gil over there? I took Erin's hand, scanning the crowd like a prison floodlight. By the time we reached it, I knew we wouldn't find them. Now I panicked, but I couldn't show Erin how shaken I was.

I decided to retrace our steps. In those days, there were no airport security checkpoints, so we were able to walk back down the concourse, me lugging Gil's suitcase along with Erin's. The arrival gate was deserted, lights out at the podium.

I gave Erin a thin smile. "Well hell. I wonder what happened?"

She said nothing.

Gil was fucking with me, hiding with Amy in some airport bar. He wanted me to overreact, to freak out, to weep. He wanted me to bargain with God. And when I gave up, he'd leap out as if nothing was wrong. *You're crazy, Kerry!*

We walked back to the first carousel, which was no longer turning. There were no more suitcases.

Again we waited.

Erin sat on Gil's bag, her lids drooping. She must've been so tired. Tired of being driven around, and flown around, tired of fighting and commotion, of being forced to witness the chaos of her parents' lives.

"Get up, sweetheart. I need to look in Daddy's suitcase."

She leaned against me as I placed it flat on its side. I knelt to unzip it and rifled through Gil's jeans and T-shirts, his socks and underwear. He'd wrapped a pair of brand-new white sneakers in plastic. He'd packed a leather shaving kit. Toothbrush and paste. At bottom I unearthed a computer manual, and in a zippered pocket, Gil's wallet. It contained two fifties and a Visa card in someone else's name. His own driver's license. Why would he pack his wallet? Wouldn't he need it handy? A chill ran through me. He must've been carrying alternate ID.

Also inside the zippered pocket: a plastic baggie filled with a white powder that was probably crank. *Good God*. I tossed it on top of his clothing and dropped the wallet into my purse. I zipped up the suitcase. "Let's go," I said to Erin, and aimed us toward a white security phone.

A few minutes after calling, a couple of airport police approached. The men looked like brothers, both fair-haired and young. I explained that my daughter had flown in from San Diego with her father—my ex-husband—but when we got to baggage claim, he wasn't there.

"He's got her," I said.

The officers, confused, looked at Erin.

"I'm sorry, our *other* daughter. She's three." I fished Gil's wallet from my purse and showed them his driver's license. "That's him."

"And you think . . . what?"

"He took our younger daughter."

The officers eyed Gil's suitcase. "That his?"

"Yes."

"He can't have gone far. He'll want his things."

I tried to decide whether to report the white powder; this would be the time. But what if they thought it was mine? What if, as with the dynamite on Vinnie's truck, they wondered if I'd planted it? What if Gil came strolling up, and they arrested him for possession?

"Why would he take her?" one of the officers asked.

"To get back at me."

"All right . . . You said *ex*-husband—you're divorced?"

I nodded.

"What's the arrangement on visitation?"

My heart dropped. "That hasn't been settled. We don't have a final decree."

"So you're not divorced."

I closed my eyes, lids fluttering.

"Do you have temporary custody?"

"Not officially. But the girls live with me."

I heard how it sounded.

The officer blew out his pink cheeks. "I sympathize, ma'am. But until a judge says otherwise, your husband has as much right to his daughter as you. If he—"

"Why would he want to get back at you?" the other officer asked, suspicion in his voice, and doubt. Doubt about me. I was a woman and must have done something.

Coldly I asked, "Does it matter?"

"No, ma'am." A pause. "Do you think he'd hurt your daughter?"

Oh God. It never occurred to me, though it should have. I was sweating profusely now. The officer glanced at Erin, who clung shivering to my waist.

"All right," he said, softening. He took out a notepad. I passed him Gil's driver's license, and he wrote down the number and Gil's physical description. He asked: What was Amy wearing? How tall was she? What color was her hair? How much did she weigh?

"What kind of car does he drive?"

"I don't think he has a car."

"Okay. Hang on." The officer stepped to one side and spoke into a walkie-talkie. *Custody* and *look around* and *keep an eye out*. The other officer patrolled the baggage area, peering into various corners, and under some other circumstance it might've been funny, because there was so evidently nothing and no one here.

AFTER THE AIRPORT police left, I found a phone booth and called the apartment in Santa Cruz. But it was too soon; Vinnie wasn't there. I called his LA number, thinking he might stop on the drive to pick up messages, but really, I just wanted to hear his voice on the machine. What could I say? I left it at *Get here as soon as you can.*

I set up camp near the white courtesy phone. Erin lay down and promptly fell asleep. I covered her with a sweater from Gil's suitcase and lifted her head into my lap. I leaned back against the wall. Time passed. My neck went achy, my legs numb. Security swung by to check in, but no one had seen Amy or Gil. More time passed. I dozed, awakened over and over by a muddled awareness that something was wrong. I should call the apartment again, but I couldn't leave Erin. I shook with sudden fury. *Why* did I let him get ahead of us? How could I be so stupid? And why were we still here? Gil wasn't going to magically reappear. I became convinced now that he was in Santa Cruz, waiting for us, buffing his nails, while we'd spent the entire night in the airport. Erin, once awakened, sat silent and grumpy. I got her to her feet. We dragged ourselves out into the morning sun and marched to the visitors' lot, where I dumped Gil's suitcase in the trunk. Then I drove us home.

And before I could get Erin out of the car, Vinnie was on the sidewalk. He reached into the back seat, lifted Erin, who was again asleep, and carried her inside. We put her to bed, then sat together on the loveseat. I talked until my words made no sense, weeping so hard I choked. Vinnie held me. To say a child kidnapped feels like a death dishonors losses from illness or accident or murder or act of war. But Amy's absence felt like a death. I didn't know where she was. I didn't know if she was safe. How could she be with Gil? He couldn't take care of her. He didn't even know her.

Vinnie was speaking, and standing, and pulling me up. "We should start making calls."

WE CALLED EVERY place and everyone we could think of: local airports, BART and bus stations, other airports, our families, neighbors, friends and former friends, coworkers and former bosses.

I called Gil's ex-wife Rita. In a voice taut with urgency, she said, "Erin should sleep in your bed. He'll come in through the window and take her, too." I called Bernard at our old apartment, who said he hadn't seen Gil. I called Mutti, Gil's elderly mom. She hadn't heard from him in over a year.

My attorney said, "Sit tight while I make inquiries." Within the hour he had news: there was an outstanding warrant for Gil in San Francisco, a DUI nonappearance. The attorney suggested we drive up to the city, stop at any precinct, and see if they'd help us look. In the meantime, he'd send an associate up to Marin County to apply for an emergency court order demanding Amy's return. There was an excellent chance the judge would grant me temporary custody.

Two Santa Cruz police officers stopped by the apartment. They took notes on the kidnapping, and walked through every room, their demeanor serious but unperturbed. They rattled me; it was plain they didn't like this one bit. But since I had two telephone lines, they'd ask Pacific Bell to set up a trap-and-trace—if Gil made contact, we should alert them from the second line. "Try to keep him talking as long as you can." The officer wrote the contact number for the phone company on a card and gave it to Vinnie.

"Will you listen in?" Vinnie asked.

In the movies, FBI agents always sit waiting with the family, reassuring them while operating mysterious equipment and wearing headphones. Not in this case. By law, police couldn't monitor the actual communications.

The officer said carefully, "There's nothing to stop *you* from recording."

Vinnie set out to purchase cassettes.

By the time he returned, my attorney had secured emergency custody. A hearing was scheduled for a week hence, where Gil and

I would each make our case, and the judge would decide whether to overturn the emergency order, modify it, or let it stand permanently. This sounded positive, I thought.

But what if Gil and Amy weren't found?

I COULDN'T SLEEP—how could I? Yet I did, body and soul plunged down into a well where all was darkness and, inexplicably, peace. At dawn, Erin stood by the side of the bed. She wanted breakfast— she was hungry. But first I opened the covers so she could crawl in. Sighing, she burrowed under my arm. She'd grown this past year, had knobby shoulders and knees. The big sister. What did it mean to her that Amy was gone, that the bed next to hers was empty? Did she think it was her fault? Children always do. I pulled her close. I told her how much I loved her. No one, I said, can take that away, it is forever. I told her, You can count on me.

I GOT OUT my shoebox of snapshots and pulled a few of Amy that would photocopy well. Vinnie found a clear, unmutilated one of Gil. I sat at my thrift-store typewriter and fed in paper to make a flyer. Time, place of abduction, physical descriptions. Space to paste in photos. At the bottom, I typed in our phone numbers along with the number for the Santa Cruz police.

We made hundreds of copies at Kinkos before driving Erin to the airport; Mom had convinced me to send her back to San Diego. In the parking lot, though, Erin seemed forlorn. I hesitated. Was it cruel to put her on the plane? Vinnie got us moving. He talked about the fun Erin would have seeing Grandma again. *There's a great zoo in San Diego, ask her to take you.*

We purchased a ticket at check-in. Vinnie peeled off; he'd give a stack of flyers to security. Erin and I continued on to the gate.

I finally thought to ask her: "Did Daddy say where he was going?"

She shook her head, the smallest movement.

"Sweetheart?"

Nothing.

"Did Daddy tell you his plans?"

"He wanted to take me on a plane." She said it so softly I had to duck down to hear.

"I mean once he got to San Francisco," I said. "Did he talk about where he wanted to go?"

"It was a *different* one, Mommy. At Grandma's airport."

I took her hands in mine and chafed her fingers to warm them. I looked into her eyes. "Tell me."

"We got in line for New York. I saw the sign."

"That can't be right, sweetheart—Grandma would've noticed."

"Grandma didn't come in."

"What do you mean, she didn't come in?" Then, understanding, I exploded. "Jesus Christ! Mom!"

Erin started to cry. She thought I was angry with her. "I told Daddy I didn't want to go to New York, and he got mad. He wouldn't talk to me on the plane."

"It's okay, baby. It's okay. You spoke up. You're so brave."

It registered now: Gil had tried to take Erin to New York, possibly while traveling under another identity. I shuddered. Erin had thwarted her own kidnapping, because she could read. Amy, on the other hand, didn't know her telephone number. I wasn't confident she could name the town where we lived. Why hadn't I made sure she learned these things? Because she was only a baby.

And I remembered Erin's despair last night in the concourse, watching her father carry Amy. Knowing what he'd done in San

Diego, did she intuit his next move? Did she, subconsciously, know?

We handed Erin over to a stewardess who would look out for her during the flight and, in San Diego, walk her down the gate to Mom.

Vinnie and I stood at the windows until the plane taxied away, until we were sure it was in the air.

I LAY ON TOP of the bedcovers fully dressed. Vinnie stretched out beside me. Our first day's search had yielded nothing; we'd already run out of places to look. I'd always believed I understood Gil better than anyone, but how little I'd ever known of what he did with his days, of where and with whom he spent time.

At 11 p.m. the phone rang. I leapt to my feet, certain it was Gil, but it was Mom—I'd called her earlier, our conversation just long enough to learn that Erin had safely arrived.

"The poor kid didn't want to go down, but she knocked right out." Mom was worried sick about Amy, "off who-knows-where with that maniac." She worried about me.

A car passed on the street below, headlamps beaming onto the ceiling through the bedroom windows. Hiss of tires on wet pavement. It was raining.

"Why didn't you go in?" I asked Mom.

She knew what I meant. A heavy silence descended. "We were late," she said. "There wasn't enough time to park and I got flustered. I thought it would be fine."

"Why didn't you tell me?"

"I'm sorry, Kerry."

And then, astonishingly, she sang. It was the hymn she'd tucked me into bed with long ago. *Holy God, we praise Thy Name.* Her low voice put me into a trance. My body slackened, my mind skated and slipped. What did it mean to be a mother? *Infinite Thy vast domain, Everlasting is Thy reign.*

THE NEXT DAY Vinnie and I went up to San Francisco, to SFPD's Northern Station on Fillmore Street, where we met with a uniformed officer and explained the situation. Another officer joined us, computer printout in hand. "We can drive you around some," he said. "Help you look. The warrant means that if we find them"— he waved the printout—"we can arrest your husband."

In the station's lot the officers guided us into the back of a black-and-white. There were no door handles inside and a metal grate divided us from the front. This vehicle was a jail on wheels. Hard not to feel we were the ones in trouble.

The officers asked where Gil might be. "Does he work in the city?"

"He doesn't have a job," Vinnie said.

"What about friends?"

I explained that the last I'd known, his friends were fellow salesmen at an art gallery downtown, where he no longer worked. But I'd already spoken to them.

Traffic clogged the streets. The sidewalks teemed with pedestrians. Homeless people, mostly men, sat upright against buildings, or slept on cardboard, layered in clothing and dirty blankets. Trolleys climbed the hills. From the back of the patrol car I looked into as many passing faces as possible. I loved San Francisco, all its nooks and crannies, but now any one might hide Amy and Gil. Four hundred thousand people lived in this city, with over a million in the greater Bay Area, and millions more in the rest of California. Even if Amy and Gil were still in the state, how would we ever find them?

Vinnie leaned forward to ask, "In cases like this, what do you usually do?"

"We talk to friends. We check to see if there's been a report of a suspicious-looking man with a child. Does your husband have a history of violence?"

"He owns a gun," I said.

Over the radio, the dispatcher's voice crackled then faded.

"Would he use it?"

"He might," Vinnie said.

The other officer asked matter-of-factly, "What about molestation? Your daughter—"

"No," I said. "He'd never—" I stopped myself short. My inability to imagine what Gil might do had led us to this.

The officer driving pulled over to look again at the printout. "There isn't much here to work with, oh . . . someone called in from a rooming house on Potrero Hill. A man with a young kid checked in. The clerk said the kid was crying in a way that didn't sound right." *Oh Amy.* My heart was thudding. We crossed Market Street and zig-zagged east, and then climbed Potrero Hill. Near the top, the officer at the wheel double-parked and opened his door.

"We'll just wait here," the other officer said.

A wooden staircase led up to a ramshackle portico where flowering vines trailed over fluted columns. The officer stood at the front door and rang the bell, his hand on his gun belt. Someone opened up, and he stepped inside.

Vinnie and I waited for what seemed like forever, pressed against each other, hands gripped tightly, but when the officer emerged he was alone. I tried hard not to cry as he skipped down the steps and climbed back in the car. "They checked out last night." He started the engine. "Anyway, it wasn't your guy. The kid was a boy."

My God. Another child at the mercy of an adult. Another child out of reach.

Now we drove up and down one-way streets. The officers wanted to help, but there wasn't much they could do. We rolled through the Embarcadero and North Beach, into Chinatown at Washington and Mason and out the gate at Grant Avenue. Dispatch blared and we turned onto Bush, heading west. If Vinnie and I couldn't suggest specific places to look, the officers needed to get back to the station.

In the lot, they hit the door locks and freed us. They were sorry they couldn't be of more assistance, but they'd watch for incoming reports, and if something came up they'd look into it. We thanked them. We all shook hands. They wished us luck.

Luck.

The next day we drove up to San Rafael for the emergency custody hearing. Gil was unsurprisingly a no-show. My attorney's associate greeted us in the corridor. In the courtroom, he made a short presentation. The judge asked me a few questions, but there was no one to speak for Gil. I left with a sole custody order, the entire proceeding over in ten minutes flat.

WE STUCK CLOSE to home now. All we could do was wait for Gil to phone. He *had* to phone.

In the girls' room, I sat on Amy's rumpled bed, her stuffed animals strewn all around. A stack of folded laundry, her T-shirts and sweatpants, sat on the dresser, a picture book face down beside them. I'd been reading to Amy before we left to get Erin—she had to come home, so we could finish the story. Closing my eyes, I sent her messages through the ether, my mind and heart pumping, every nerve awake and on fire. I was trying to *feel* her. But I couldn't.

Goddamn it. Goddamn Gil.

Over the next several days I grew prickly, itchy, angry, increas-ingly unwilling to be consoled. Did Vinnie understand? I didn't know. When Amy had been gone for eight days, I left our vigil to head out alone for some air. I walked several blocks, calmly, then briskly, then in a cold sweat I ran back to the apartment, convinced I'd missed Gil's call. I found Vinnie crying. He tried to hide it. Something terrible must've happened, the police must've phoned. But no. His tears were private. He was confronting his own guilt, and his fears. Gil had taken Amy because Vinnie wanted me—because he wanted *us*. And now the woman he loved had lost her child, and that child was in danger.

Vinnie's cheeks felt hot under my hands. His lips were dry, small rips in the skin where he'd bitten them. I kissed him, a grave kiss, weighted with all that felt inexpressible. I was so grateful for him. Gil would be crazed whether I was with Vinnie, or someone else, or no one. My real crime was that I'd rejected him.

I watched myself as if from a distance.

The adulteress.

The runaway wife.

The grieving mother.

I knew what I'd done and what I deserved. It wasn't this.

ON THE TENTH day, Gil called.

Vinnie alerted the phone company from the second line.

And pressed RECORD.

9

The Stolen Bicycle

Forty-five minutes. That's how long I kept Gil talking. When it was over, Vinnie rewound the tape and pressed PLAY. He wanted to make sure we'd gotten it all.

Gil's first words: *So, what's new?*

Mine: *Let me talk to Amy.*

I gasped. "Turn it off."

Vinnie hit STOP.

"I can't listen to it." The sound of our voices terrified me.

Vinnie removed the tape from the recorder. "Look. Kerry. It's out."

Later, I buried this recording at the bottom of my strongbox. There it would remain for the next twenty years.

The cops called to discuss the trace. Over those forty-five minutes, Pacific Bell had followed the signal northward, from one antique switching station to the next. I'd assumed I'd kept him on long enough, but the phone company couldn't pinpoint Gil's location. The best they could do was the name of the town: Santa Rosa, about sixty miles north of San Francisco.

It didn't matter, though. Because I'd told Gil what he wanted to hear. I would give up Vinnie. And Gil would return Amy to me.

It was the only part of the conversation I'd ever recall with accuracy.

I will give up Vinnie.

I meant the words when I said them, while also understanding that I was lying. There was no reconciling this conflict. I wanted my daughter—she belonged with me. But I would not give up Vinnie. I would not abandon him or the commitment we'd made to each other.

Did Gil hear it in my voice?

For his part, did he mean what he said about giving back Amy? Or was he lying, too?

We arranged to meet in downtown San Francisco the following night, at 8:30 p.m., at the corner of Eddy and Hyde. I scribbled down the information. The scratch of my pencil sounded like the panting of a tiny animal.

"No cops," Gil warned, like a kidnapper in a movie.

"I wouldn't. I won't."

"I mean it. Come alone, Kerry."

The police wouldn't like this, and who could blame them? They'd wasted time on a situation where a woman had, as women so often do in domestic conflicts, changed her mind. But if Gil sensed I was lying about this, I knew he'd vanish for good with Amy.

I caught Vinnie's eye. He nodded grimly.

Speaking carefully into the receiver, "No cops," I agreed.

EDDY WAS ONE-WAY going east, and as I approached the intersection with Hyde, which was also one-way, I drove slowly in the right lane. The night was foggy and the street poorly lit, which fed my anxiety. I looked for Amy and Gil on all four corners but saw nothing and no one—why hadn't we specified precisely where they would be? Vehicles piled up behind me. Someone leaned on a horn, and I rolled through the intersection cursing. Partway down the next block, I pulled over. I got out and stood on the sidewalk peering back through the shifting mist. It was cold, the sky a yellowish gray. All four corners at Hyde and Eddy stood empty. I might've walked back and waited for them there, but I couldn't leave the car. My intention was to collect Amy and *go*. I got behind the wheel and crept forward, eyes flicking to the rearview.

A lean shadow took shape in the mirror.

Behind me, another horn blared, and high beams blinded me. Cursing again, I sped up. I passed Leavenworth, a one-way in the wrong direction. *Fuck*. At Jones I made a right. Another right at Turk. I bypassed Leavenworth on the way back to Hyde. By the time I completed the circuit I was dry-mouthed and drenched in sweat, furious at myself for not having checked a map in advance. In those few precious minutes, Gil could have decided I'd called the police after all. Maybe it was a huge mistake not having them here. Maybe Gil and Amy were already away. Gone.

But no. There they were on the northeast corner, Gil slouched against the side of a building, holding Amy.

I moved through the intersection, pulled over, and stopped short, prompting another horn. Through the windshield I watched Gil shake his head. I left the engine running and threw open the door, jumped out and ran around to the sidewalk.

Amy saw me. "Mommy! Mommy!"

A rush of adrenaline. I was blazing with joy. The light in her face undid me. She kicked her heels and reached out, but when I rushed forward to take her, Gil tightened his hold.

I stepped in close, wormed my arms and hands between them, and tried to wrest her free. Gil's shoulders loosened. The hand on Amy's back slackened. He seemed prepared to let go, but at the crucial moment he twisted away. Amy turned her head to follow me.

She thought we were playing. I tried again, and again Gil twisted away. Was this fun for him? I didn't want a tug of war. I didn't want to frighten Amy.

She still had on the knitted jacket she was wearing when he'd taken her, but the threaded pink ribbons were missing; he'd pulled them from their eyelets. Gil noted me noticing. He pulled back the jacket's hood, and I vibrated with shock: he'd cropped her feathery blonde curls close and dyed her hair brown. To change her. To disguise her. She looked like a little boy.

"How do you like them apples, Kerry?"

My knees shook. Don't cry. *Don't cry.*

"How could you?" I croaked.

Gil shrugged. He pressed his cheek to Amy's, mugging. Her round cheeks were mine, her curly lips his, her blue eyes and delicate chin her own.

"Guess where we spent the first few nights?" he asked. "Amy knows. Don't you, monkey?" I stared stupidly, and he said, "The Grant Hotel? On Bush? Remember it, Kerry?"

I did. Years ago, we'd stayed at the Grant while looking for a rental before moving north. Good God. All that driving around with SFPD. It never occurred to me he'd hide in a place he might be found.

"Had to stick her in the shower to rinse the dye out." Gil chuckled. "She shrieked like a banshee. Whew. I thought the SWAT team would bust through a window."

Amy hated the shower, but he wouldn't know. He hadn't bathed her since she was a baby.

"We were gonna go back to the airport," he said. "But I thought maybe they'd be looking for me. Made me a little paranoid, if you want to know the truth. So we went somewhere else."

I wanted to say, *Yeah, Santa Rosa.* That would wipe the grin off his face.

"Mommy." Amy again held out her arms. She kicked her heels, but less forcefully. She giggled when Gil smooched her ear.

"Not yet, monkey."

I couldn't stand another second. "Gil, please. Please give her to me." I reached for my daughter, again, forcing my arms between them. Gil's jacket hung open, and I imagined I felt his heart beating. His breath warmed my forehead—he was wheezing. I pulled Amy toward me, Gil pulled her away. It sickened me. No one would win here, no one could win, there was no winning.

"Did you mean what you said?" Gil asked. "What you promised me?"

"Yes," I said.

"You won't see Vinnie anymore, right? You won't call him. You won't talk to him ever again. Right? You promised me."

"Yes."

"Say it."

"I won't see Vinnie again."

Gil loosened his grip on Amy. "I'm moving to Santa Cruz," he said. "To make sure you keep that promise."

No, no, no, no.

"I gotta be where I can keep an eye on you. I'm telling you, Kerry, if you break your promise, there's gonna be hell to pay. You won't be able to live with yourself. You get what I mean?"

"I do."

"You sure? Think before you answer."

"I get it," I said firmly.

"Again."

"I get it. I get it. Gil! Please! Give her to me."

He let go, and Amy toppled into my arms. The contours of her little body. The weight. I smelled dried tears on her cheeks and wanted to lick them away. I hugged her to my breast. But it was too much, too hard, too tight, and she wailed.

"*Kerry*," Gil said. I glanced at him—he'd lifted the bottom edge of his shirt. "Look here."

A tightly cinched belt. A strip of pale belly. The butt of a gun sticking up from his waistband.

My God. That fucking gun. He'd carried that thing next to Amy.

"Had it in the car at Hamburger Hamlet," he said. "I was gonna stick it in Vinnie's mouth and pull the trigger."

I took a lurching step, then rushed to the car and fumbled one-handed with the rear passenger door. Behind me I heard Gil snorting. Was he coming after us? My heart clutched. I was so horribly afraid. When I got the door open, I dropped Amy into her car seat and frantically buckled her up. I ran into the street and around to the driver's side door. Seated, I gripped the steering wheel so tightly my hands numbed. Through the windshield I saw Gil's bottom half; he was back to leaning against the building. I looked over a shoulder at Amy, who stared out the window.

As I pulled into the lane she cried out, "Daddy! Daddy!"

AT A DINER several blocks away, bells strung to the front door jangled when we entered. Vinnie sat waiting in a booth in the back. When he saw us, he slid out and leapt up. Strode forward. He wrapped his arms around me and my child, his chest heaving. And he wept. He pulled back to look at Amy, touched her hair, and stared at me in wonder. Amy patted Vinnie's wet face, her own tears forgotten.

We stumbled to the booth, where the three of us squeezed in on the same side. I snugged up against the wall; Amy stood on the banquette between Vinnie and me. Should Vinnie be on the end like this, so he could get out quickly and defend me and Amy? Or should I be? What would make it easier to get Amy safely away? Or were we all trapped anyway? We faced the front door, with a view to the entrance and through the window out to the street, and I would do this for many years to come, like a mobster expecting a hit. A waitress brought menus and a booster seat for Amy, and my girl, knowing the drill, climbed right on. The diner was warm, the air steamy and fragrant with cooking smells. I freed Amy from her jacket.

Vinnie couldn't stop staring at her hair. "It's like he painted a stolen bicycle."

We ordered grilled cheese sandwiches, french fries, and chocolate shakes. I was hungrier than I'd ever been in my life, but once the food arrived I couldn't eat. I watched Vinnie watching Amy. Comically, he stuffed himself for her entertainment. She smeared her delighted face with melted cheese. Her short, newly dark hair stood on end, and her eyes were bleary. She should've been home in Santa Cruz, in bed, fast asleep. She lunged across the table, knocking over her glass of milk; it was her signature move, and I laughed. She wanted to stand again in the booth. She wanted to get down. She wanted to sing. *Twinkle, twinkle, little star.* I marveled at her resilience, but damage, I knew, had been done. My job now was to protect my daughters forever.

But first, and right this second, I had to talk to Mom. Released from the table, I made for the phone booth back by the ladies'. I dialed Mom's number and she answered on the first ring. When I told her we had Amy, she said over and over, "Thank God." She woke Erin up and put her on the phone.

"Your sister is home," I said. "We're coming down to Grandma's with Amy."

After a long silence Erin said quietly, "He didn't want me."

Imagine scaring one child out of her wits. Imagine making her feel unloved, then taking the other child and camouflaging her identity.

"*I* want you," I told her. "*I* love you. I'm coming tomorrow. And Vinnie's coming, and Amy. Okay, sweetheart? We're all coming."

When I returned to the table, I slid in across from Vinnie and Amy. I folded my hands, and lifted my chin, and held Vinnie's gaze before saying, "We have to run."

10

The Spies Who Came in to the Cold

Two weeks into our family's new life in Boulder, Colorado, the real estate agent who'd traded us painting for a month's rent stopped by the condo to check on our progress and chat. This soon became a regular thing: he'd show up with pastries, and we'd make coffee. Vinnie and I recognized that, from the agent's point of view, if we felt welcome we might do a better job; from ours, if we did a good job and, more importantly, if we reliably presented as "normal"—which, given how traumatized we were, and how paranoid, wasn't easy—maybe he'd let us stay.

When he asked why we'd left California, we coughed up a short version: rough divorces and the desire to start again. The agent was himself divorced, no need to say anything more.

Did we plan to stay in Boulder?

We did.

We must've looked like people who, while clearly not rich, might want to purchase a house. The real estate agent offered to tour us around. We didn't know how to say no.

He piloted his Jeep at a crawl through neighborhoods: South Boulder, North Boulder, Whittier, Gunbarrel, The Hill. Vinnie sat up front, the girls and I in the back. The Rockies jutted to the west; to the east, the prairie opened wide. The agent pointed out landmarks and told stories about growing up in this town. "It's a great place for families," he said. Driving over a bridge, we looked down on a creek, picnickers on the banks, teenagers in inner tubes float-ing past. Boulder wasn't that different from California, but I already missed the ocean. I missed my friends, and my job. Most of all, I missed my mom.

The desire to talk to her was overwhelming. Since arriving in Colorado we'd spoken just once, when I called from a phone booth in downtown Denver. The first thing out of my mouth had been "Are you okay?" The question hung there in all its ridiculous inad-equacy. My mother was a widow and I her only child. How could I have left her? But "I'm *fine*," she reassured me. "What about you?" Mom's voice conjured her physical self, her short blonde hair cut like a man's and her tired blue eyes. When young she'd been an elegant dresser, but in retirement she favored baggy pedal pushers and T-shirts and plastic slides. I pictured her with her feet up on the coffee table, a crumpled tissue stuffed in her bra, a burning ciga-rette in one hand. We talked about the girls. Nothing big, nothing important. Nothing that anyone eavesdropping could identify. Her longing came down the line. It was unbearable. I said cautiously, "Anything?" Meaning Gil. I imagined him incandescent with fury that we'd disappeared. Had he contacted Mom? Had he harassed or threatened or abused her? Was he telephoning over and over, as he'd done with me for more than a year? The police, I knew from experience, would do nothing until it was too late. And I was the one who'd put her in this situation.

"Not a peep," Mom said.

I heard an echo, a small change in the call's quality. My breath caught. Was he . . . could he have tapped her phone? Was that even possible? Reading my mind, Mom said quickly, "Don't tell me where you are." What a kindness, I thought. As if me shutting her out was her idea. I exhaled, feeling helpless, and crushed by shame.

From the back of the Jeep, I considered Vinnie's neck, burnt red by Colorado's high-altitude sun. The girls on either side of me stared out the windows. Soft summer air gusted. Colors shined too bright. Spending time with the real estate agent like this unnerved me—I felt tongue-tied and on guard. Still, I had to admit it was pleasant to be ferried about.

Pleasant, as well, to wander through houses for sale.

This was before the staging that is so common now; many homes were crammed with artwork and books, sports equipment, clothing, and toys, these belongings provoking speculation about other lives. Some houses stood empty, tempting you to imagine them as your own. The girls ran in and out of bedrooms, already choosing which would be theirs. "This is the right time to buy," the agent said. "Prices are going to rise."

Vinnie and I exchanged a loaded glance. We could not buy a house, because legally we didn't exist. We were wasting the agent's time. But we said nothing.

JULY BECAME AUGUST. We finished painting the condo and paid rent for the following month. We allowed ourselves to hope. On evening walks over to Longs, the air felt newly chilled, the odd yellow leaf peeking out from dusty greenery. Soon the school year would start. We couldn't put it off any longer. We had to enroll the girls.

We chose Sacred Heart, Boulder's only Catholic grammar school. If we signed up as new members of the parish, maybe faked baptismal certificates would suffice in terms of paperwork. We found a religious supply store in Denver, purchased blank forms, and using the girls' originals as models, filled in false information by hand.

In the school administrator's office, I said I'd home-taught but now needed to go back to work—the second part of that assertion, at least, was true. Vinnie handed over the forged baptismal certificates. The administrator did not bat an eye. Erin was given a placement test and assigned to third grade, while Amy would attend preschool. We emerged from the meeting stunned. It felt too easy.

The first day of class, after we dropped them off and all the other parents had left, Vinnie and I remained in our car parked across the street from the school. He held my hand.

"We can just sit here," he said.

I loved him for it—we both knew he was due at his job. He'd been hired at a futon shop that served the town's student population, the owner wanting to expand into furniture finishing; Vinnie, who'd been scouring the classifieds, answered the ad. The owner had agreed to pay cash under the table, no surprise, as the place was rife with dubious characters, near-hermits and workers who walked off the job without warning, sometimes with tools or money from the cash register. Vinnie's first day of work, he'd arrived to find the furniture stripper squatted in a corner near containers of noxious chemicals, smoking a joint. Vinnie made him put it out. "Fuckin' narc," the guy complained. Vinnie laughed. "You can blow yourself up if you want, but you're not taking me with you."

In the car, he said, "The girls will be fine. I promise."

I drove him to the shop, then returned to the condo. Alone for the first time in weeks, I didn't know what to do with myself. *Ordinary life.* I said it aloud. It was all we'd dreamed of, when we ran.

I did laundry and read the *Daily Camera*: local news, the crime blotter, the weather forecast, the want ads. I thought about my husband making old furniture beautiful. And the girls? What were they learning? Would it be hard for them to make friends? I was glad they had each other, even if they were stuck in separate classrooms. When I fetched them at the end of that day, I hugged them both hard. And in the car they fell into one of those zero-sum sibling wars, full of grievance. I yelled at them and felt bad for yelling. They scuffled one last time before settling sullenly. This, too, was ordinary life.

MID-FALL, THE REAL estate agent called to tell us he'd sold the condo. Potential buyers had come through periodically, so we'd known that a sale was inevitable, but the news still upended me. Where would we go now? Where else could we live without identifying papers? What other landlord would be so understanding? The agent said he'd keep an eye out for another rental. He paused. What he really thought we should do was take a second look at a house he'd shown us weeks ago, a Tudor-style Craftsman a few blocks west of the university. The owner was a professor in Pasadena, California, a woman who'd grown sick of being a long-distance landlord. The house had sat empty for a year. "She's a motivated seller," he said, code for "willing to lower the price."

The house's yard was overgrown, the inside as dreary as I remembered. "Take a thousand off for every month on the market," the agent said. "Plus five for the roof. I know someone who can fix it for half that. I'm telling you, this place is a steal." The price was a third of what something similar would cost in California.

Vinnie and I stepped into a tiny front room. He waved his arms at the heavy shelves nailed over dark wood paneling. "I can take down this wall."

I saw that he wanted it more than I did. All his adult life he'd been a renter. He'd never thought he'd own a home.

"I think he's a friend," Vinnie said. He meant the real estate agent. "I bet he'd help us."

"Help us how?"

"I don't know. Something."

Vinnie was a more optimistic person than me, and harder to shake, but given our circumstances it all felt dangerous. Disclosure might even be lethal. We didn't really know this man. How could we trust him? But Vinnie had risked everything for me and the girls. He'd given up his life in Los Angeles, his business, his family. His parents didn't even know where he was. How much loss could he be expected to take?

"Let's explain it a bit more," he said. "See what happens."

"Okay," I agreed.

Seated in the real estate agent's office, we told him about the stalking, the kidnapping and death threats. We told him we'd changed our names, and that we were in hiding. "We can't get a mortgage, but we have cash," Vinnie said. "Might be enough for a down payment. Is there some other way?"

The agent flopped back in his chair, thinking. Maybe, he said, the professor would carry the loan. It would be a good deal for her: If we defaulted, she'd keep the house, along with our down payment. He then withdrew to the lobby so that Vinnie and I could discuss this. Vinnie thought it sounded fine. I was warier, afraid of losing the only financial cushion we had.

"What if this is our one chance?" he said.

And I saw again how much he wanted it. I threw an arm around his neck and pressed my lips to his throat. "Okay," I murmured. "Okay."

We waved the agent back in. He drew up the offer. We signed, and he faxed it to Pasadena.

Two days later, he called us to come in and see him. We sat behind a glass wall that looked over the reception area. The girls were out there playing hide-and-seek, though there were limited places to hide.

The professor had accepted our offer. All she needed now was a copy of our credit report.

Vinnie and I shook our heads. We could not provide a credit report, because we would not reveal our real names.

The real estate agent sighed. He suggested calling the professor again; this time he'd put us on speakerphone. "Just tell her exactly what you told me about your ex-husband. Who knows? It might make a difference."

After introductions and some stilted small talk, the professor said, "So. What's the story?"

Vinnie did the talking. His spoke calmly, and reasonably, but laid out like this—over speakerphone, to a woman we'd never met—it all sounded crazy.

When he'd finished, I leaned toward the phone and added: "We can't risk it."

Into the ensuing silence the professor said, "What's really going on here? Are you drug dealers?"

"No," Vinnie said.

"Growers always have cash," she said.

The accusation disoriented me. It felt true, somehow, a road we'd taken without being aware.

"These are good folks," the agent jumped in.

How would he know?

"If you don't want to do it," Vinnie said, "we understand. We'll walk away. But if you do accept this, please, please never tell anyone about us. People talk. It's a small world."

We'd come to the end of this venture, I thought. It was a relief. I turned then to Vinnie only to see emotions scudding like clouds over his face: disappointment, sadness, resignation.

"All right," the professor said, "I'll do it. I'll carry the loan."

She then told us a story. Some years ago, she'd gone on safari to photograph wildlife in the African bush. Each night for a week, seven strangers had passed whiskey around a campfire and made confessions under the stars. A young woman had talked about a long-distance affair, recounting a first, comically unsuccessful sexual encounter at an academic conference, and then—the woman was drunk, she could not stop herself—detailing an increasingly reckless passion. The man, who was married, would not divorce. When the young woman threatened to tell his wife, he broke off the affair. He would not risk losing his kids.

The professor's voice softened. "That man? I recognized him as one of my colleagues. What were the odds?" She paused. "It is a small world."

The day of the closing, we dropped the girls off at school, went to the real estate agent's office to sign documents and pick up the key, then drove straight to the house. We climbed the porch to the front door. Vinnie ran his finger over the brass nameplate, THE HIRSHBERGS, the former owner's last name. I touched the mezuzah fixed to the doorframe. It was like the house had been waiting for us, all dressed up in a phony ID. "We should keep both," I said. Vinnie put the key in the lock and pushed open the door. He kissed me and swept me up and carried me in.

We walked through dark, empty rooms. The walls were grimy. The kitchen ceiling sagged. The carpet in the stairwell stank of cat piss. *Home.* It was overwhelming.

We lingered in the dining room, the prettiest spot in the house, though Virginia creeper blocked its south-facing windows. In June the leaves had been green, but now they held a ruby tinge. Along one wall, a mirror set into the built-in china cabinet dimly winked. The silvering was mottled and peeled away from the edges, and our murky reflections looked like revenants. The hair at the back of my neck stood on end.

"What are you thinking?" Vinnie asked.

"I don't know, I don't know," I said.

"Wait," he said.

He went out the front. I saw movement beyond the creeper, then the ocean blue of his shirt, his arms reaching to tear down the vines.

THE HOUSE, BUILT in 1920 of brick and stone and half-timbered stucco, was mostly solid but, as we discovered, not without flaws. The foundation had settled and cracks laced through the brick-work. Whenever it was windy, shingles flew from the roof like departing birds. On Christmas Eve a pipe burst, flooding the base-ment and leaving us without water. We'd spent all our savings—our cash in a bag—to buy the place and could barely afford a plumber to repair this disaster, let alone adequate heat. When temperatures dropped, all the inside surfaces radiated an iron cold. The four of us would eat dinner in coats, hats, and gloves, Vinnie joking that we were the spies who came in *to* the cold. Then, no matter how ridiculously early the hour, we went upstairs to bed.

I interviewed for office jobs, finding, as I expected, that, unlike at Paladin Press, most companies wanted references and, prefera-bly, a degree. I received no offers. I suspected I put people off; under pressure, I was agitated and evasive, and I probably didn't seem very bright. After a couple of months, I became desperate. Vinnie's job at the futon shop didn't pay well, and we were always broke. The next step was competing with high schoolers and college stu-dents for food-service work.

Our real estate agent intervened to save me. He knew I'd once worked as a typographer for a commercial art studio, so he passed on my name to a few clients that needed graphic design. I offered a whopping discount for cash and was soon busy. Vinnie converted our small breakfast room into a studio. We bought a used drafting table, a T-square, a clamp-on lamp, and a rolling stool. A cabinet found in an alley on trash day held art pens and pencils and India ink, masking tape and X-Acto knives and rubber cement.

We'd delayed long enough. We needed ID. I set about forging new birth certificates for Vinnie and me.

Seated at the drafting table, I angled the lamp over our original documents. Mine, issued by the State of California, was holographic, with whorls of pink and blue ink to discourage counterfeiting. Vinnie's looked more promising. New York State had issued a simple five-by-eight photostat, the top half reversed, with white type on a solid black background. I brought it over to Kinko's and made copies to use as a base document. On a rented typewriter I tapped out the names of parents not ours, of addresses where we'd never lived.

In my old life I'd been Kerry, but now I was "Karen," a name picked because it was common (decades into the future it would become code for a woman who uses her whiteness and class privilege to steamroll those around her; if only I'd known). The girls and I shared my new last name, "Palmer," also common, and close enough to my real maiden name to cover any slip-ups mid-signature. Vinnie had chosen his new surname similarly, and where once he'd been Vincent John, he was now "John Vincent." But we told everyone to call him Vinnie.

I ordered reverse photostats from various graphics shops around town, a line here, a line there. Back at the drafting table, I sliced up the type. My hands shook, so I went to the kitchen sink and ran hot water over them until the joints loosened and my skin turned bright red, and then I sat again and finished the cuts. I coated the back of the type strips with rubber cement and dropped them into place on the base documents. Once the cement dried, I inked the cut edges so they wouldn't show up on photocopies as telltale white lines. Returning to Kinko's, I copied the doctored certificates onto different paper stocks I'd bought at an art store, trying to get as close as possible to the glossy look and feel of Vinnie's original.

We'd purchased an embosser from a company mentioned in our guide to changing identity, sending a money order through the mail. The stamp was a cartoonishly inaccurate New York State seal. A quick, lopsided squeeze imprinted it in the lower right-hand corner of both certificates.

After the girls went to bed, I laid out my handiwork on the dining-room table on either side of Vinnie's original.

We scrutinized the documents in silence. They looked good, I thought.

"Our names," Vinnie said, "they're too close to the old ones. Seeing them next to each other like this . . . If *he* ever does, he'll know it's us."

Too late now. The girls were settled in school. We'd bought a damn house. We had jobs. In consternation, I stared at my new name. *Karen Palmer.* Vinnie was right. It was too close to the original. Yet the woman I'd once been was a ghost, detectable only inside our family and in the brief interludes when I talked to Mom.

I felt so strange. I was still me, a mother, a daughter, a wife; a person who'd rather read than eat, who feared heights and drove fast, who was indifferent to fashion and allergic to housework but craved beauty and order. All my life I'd been an introvert who liked people. That hadn't changed. Yet I felt altered to the core.

Karen Palmer was a construct, a fake. I did not believe in her. Why should anyone else?

And then I remembered something Gil used to tell me. *You are who you say you are.* It is the language of con men, of fiction and affirmations and amnesia. But maybe, this once, his voice in my ear could help me; it might show me how to become someone else. The irony would have incensed him.

I turned to Vinnie. "What do you think of them?"

He lifted the certificates to the light, first mine, then his. He held the paper's edge and rubbed the embossed seals between forefinger and thumb.

"You're my favorite forger," he said.

My face went hot with pleasure that instantly turned to horror. Forgery! If we took these certificates out into the world, it would be a criminal act.

They looked almost exactly alike, I saw now—of course they did. I'd used the same paper for each, and the same typescript. The name of the hospital was the same, and the town. There were so many kinds of certificates, and this had seemed the easiest way. I could do them over, but maybe that wasn't necessary. Vinnie and I could go to Social Security weeks apart, and apply at different offices. And there, face to face with government representatives, we'd have to explain ourselves, because people in their thirties usually already had cards.

"The girls need certificates, too," I said. And Social Security numbers. April fifteenth would be upon us before we knew it. If you wanted the deduction—which we did; we needed it—dependents now had to have their own numbers. I'd have to come up with different paperwork for Erin and Amy, because for children of their generation, old-style documents wouldn't fly.

"Taxes, ugh," I said.

Vinnie groaned. "Let's worry about that later."

We sagged against each other, our courage jointly evaporating. The difficulties in getting through these last steps to complete new identities seemed insurmountable. I slid our counterfeit birth certificates into an envelope, sealed it up, and stowed it away in a drawer.

11

Most Wanted

Later that winter, I lay in bed one night watching TV. Vinnie was curled up at my side, snoring softly, sound asleep under a pile of blankets. Down the hall, the girls were also asleep. All four of us were safe in the house and safe in our beds, doubly cocooned.

I snugged the blanket more securely under my chin. Light emanating from the TV shined blue.

John Walsh, host of *America's Most Wanted*, was up on the screen.

Since moving to Boulder, I'd developed a wolfish taste for true crime. In short order I read Truman Capote's *In Cold Blood,* Joe McGinniss's *Fatal Vision*, Norman Mailer's *The Executioner's Song*, and Ann Rule's *Small Sacrifices*. "It's all so dark," Vinnie said, worrying. But to me these stories were a way to keep track of Gil, as if all criminals were alike and our survival depended on my understanding. I'd highlight points of recognition, anything that justified the decision to run. Or maybe it was only that in the suspiciously calm aftermath of our disappearance, I, like my daughters, with their attachment to *The Monster at the End of This Book*, sought horror followed by resolution.

America's Most Wanted had a different effect. From the lurid opening credits—a wide, darting blue eye and frantically ringing telephones—each episode of the show vaulted me into gnawing hypervigilance. By definition the narratives lacked endings: the bad guys remained at large, and John Walsh needed our help to catch them. Walsh had lost his six-year-old son Adam in a brutal kidnap and murder in 1981. His moral standing was beyond doubt. I could not look away.

That night, Walsh updated viewers on the case of John List.

On November 9, 1971, List, a forty-six-year-old New Jersey bank manager and devout Lutheran, had murdered his entire family. He shot his wife, Helen, while she drank her morning coffee, then climbed the stairs to an attic apartment and shot his mother, Alma. He shot Patricia and Fred, two of his three teenaged children, as they came home from school. List's eldest, John Jr., who was his favorite, died last, collected by his father from soccer practice and ambushed in the kitchen.

List dragged the bodies into the house's empty ballroom and laid them out on sleeping bags. He covered their faces with handkerchiefs.

He drove to the post office to stop the mail and at the bank made a final withdrawal. Returning home, he fixed himself lunch. He wrote letters and made phone calls, explaining that the family was leaving town ahead of the Thanksgiving holiday to care for an ailing relative. He then composed a five-page confession addressed to his pastor. List was in dire and escalating financial straits, tortured by his inability to support his family. The prospect of losing their mansion, and potentially being forced to go on welfare, was the last straw.

He went off to bed.

In the morning he scissored himself out of photographs. He turned off the heat but left the lights on. He chose music to play in a loop over the house's intercom. On his way out he locked all the doors. He drove his car to JFK airport and abandoned it. Then he disappeared.

List traveled west to Denver, Colorado, where he rented a trailer for cash. Choosing for himself the name Robert Peter "Bob" Clark, he applied for a new Social Security card. He found a job as a night cook at a Holiday Inn, then took a better job cooking at the Pinery Country Club, all the while accumulating the documentation Americans need to live: a telephone company account, a driver's license, a bank account, and charge cards. He joined a church, met and married a fellow congregant. By all accounts in Denver, Bob Clark was a quiet, decent, and unassuming man.

Eventually, he eased back into accounting. His ability to do the work, however, hadn't improved, and his finances deteriorated in ways that must have felt all too familiar. In 1988, offered a new position in Virginia, he jumped at the chance to start again, and he and his wife moved to Richmond.

When investigators approached *America's Most Wanted* about featuring the List case, the lack of a current photograph made the producers reluctant to take it on. The crime was too cold, the chances of solving it slim. But on a hunch they tried something new; they hired forensic artist Frank Bender to sculpt an age-progressed bust of John List.

Bender, working with a criminal psychologist, speculated that a numbers man with a rigid personality would balk at changes to his appearance. So Bender stuck to normal aging: balding, jowls, and thick black glasses. He made sure a long scar from an old mastoid surgery was visible. Bender dressed the bust in a dark suit jacket and striped tie.

When the segment aired in May 1989, cameras displayed the sculpture from every angle, John List in 3D brought to life. A woman watching in Denver recognized her former neighbor Bob Clark and called the hotline. List was arrested in Virginia and extradited to New Jersey. Police matched his fingerprints to the original crime scene, but List still insisted Bob Clark was his real name.

After eighteen long years, it must have felt like the truth.

I switched off the TV, suddenly compelled to check on the girls.

Amy had kicked free of her covers. My baby lay flat on her back, arms flung wide in abandon. Books and stuffed animals surrounded her, along with a small brass cat we used downstairs as a doorstop. I moved the cat to the floor and pulled up her blankets. Wispy blonde strands lay over her forehead and cheek. I stroked them away. She'd only recently begun to sleep through the night. At the condo by Longs, the four of us had shared a bedroom, and she'd often awakened in the small hours, sweaty, miserable, and crying for Daddy, her voice thick with longing or fear. I'd hold her until she grew quiet again. Sometimes, Vinnie wanted to be the one to soothe her, to be her father, and I'd let go reluctantly, afraid she'd reject him. But she'd wrap her arms around his neck and cling. By morning she'd have forgotten it all. She seemed to have no memory of the past, of California or anyone we'd left behind. Six months is a lifetime to a waking child, but I was certain her father lived in her dreams. Which father, though? The good one, who sometimes fretted over every sniffle, or the bad one, who'd kidnapped her out of my arms?

Since we'd disappeared, I'd thought a lot about whether Gil was capable of hurting Amy physically, or even killing her, as John List had done. Some men did murder their children, out of fury or despair, to make a statement or get back at their wives. Others killed themselves along with their entire families. It gave me nightmares, deranged epics in which Gil stalked us, forever trying to get *in*. I'd race through the house seconds ahead of him, locking all the windows and doors, and once I was certain everything was secure, I'd then remember a single, overlooked point of entry and know that our lives were done.

Sometimes, I felt his presence. I'd see him in a burst of movement along a sidewalk, in a crewneck sweater tightening against an Adam's apple, in nimble fingers with square nails counting out change. In the car, a glimpse of a square-shaped head—a Blokkopf—ahead in traffic would make me go dangerously faint.

I went now to Erin's room and stood in the doorway, staring at the humped crescent under her quilt. I considered that she might not be there. As a teenager I used to sneak out at night, stuffing pillows into the shape of a girl. But this child was only eight. I knew she had secrets, as everyone does, but that sort of deceit had to be years away.

I studied the quilt for movement but saw none. Erin always slept peacefully. She understood what we'd done, and she remembered everything, but she never acted out, never freaked or lost her temper. From the day we'd left California, she'd struck me as preternaturally well adjusted and calm. I feared this placidity was a mask.

I sat at the edge of the bed. Her body under the covers took shape—she lay on her side, facing away. I set a hand on her hip and jostled her, as I'd done when she was new born, to verify that she breathed.

Nothing.

I leaned down and whispered her name.

"Mommy," she said, and turned.

THE NEXT DAY, I was late picking the girls up from school. Under the best of circumstances, the hour was fraught, a liminal slice of time invariably spoiled by my chronic fears. I *hated* being late. I never wanted the girls to spend a single second wondering where I was.

The temperature, which had been dropping all day, was now below freezing. Driving north on Ninth Street, I hit a patch of ice and lost control of the car. I slid up over the curb into low shrubbery. It wasn't much of a collision—I wasn't going that fast—but it shook me. I turned off the engine and gathered myself, got out, and walked around to look at the front end. It was scratched up but fine. I pushed a bit at the shrubbery, to no real purpose, shaking snow from the branches onto my boots. My hands throbbed; I'd forgotten my gloves. I looked up and down the street, peering into cars as they rolled past, expecting that square-shaped head. But the drivers were strangers, their expressions oddly inanimate. No one stopped. After a while I felt steadier. I climbed back into the driver's seat, started up, and shifted into reverse. The wheels spun. I put it in first and jolted deeper into the shrubs. Again I tried reversing, and the car shot backward into the lane. Flustered but unharmed, I drove on.

And I found myself thinking about the previous night's viewing. *John List*. If he'd wanted free of his family, why didn't he just leave? If he couldn't bear the shame of poverty, why not kill himself rather than them?

The year John List disappeared, the data bank for the FBI's new National Crime Information Center was still under construction. In 1989, when we ran, the agency reported 619,112 missing people. Of these, 2,500 simply vanished, though a small percentage were later found dead. Most people who disappear are running toward something, or away from something, or both. They seek adventure, or a fresh start free of expectations. A romance has soured. They feel trapped by conflicts or obligations, by debt or pressures at work. Unethical behavior slips into criminality, and flight seems the only way out. Occasionally, as with John List, the reason for disappearing is deeply sinister.

In 1989 children accounted for roughly half the missing, the majority being teenage runaways. Less than a hundred were stranger kidnappings, though it's what everyone thinks of first. A significant percentage were family abductions due to domestic or custody disputes. If Gil had reported our disappearance, we would have been part of that statistic. Had he? That cold winter day in Boulder, I didn't know.

I tightened my grip on the steering wheel. The sun hovered over the tops of the mountains, the foothills draped in shadow, stands of pine like black check marks in the snow. My head throbbed, an idea just out of reach. I thought about the ordinary life John List had made for himself as Bob Clark, his accounting job, his house in the suburbs, his church membership, his fucking eyeglasses. Everything normal as normal could be. Jesus Christ. I *identified* with John List.

I'd been searching for Gil in List's story, only to find myself. Because weren't Vinnie and I fugitives? Criminals, with our bag of cash and forged birth certificates. We'd left family behind— Mom, and Vinnie's parents—and it wasn't murder but it felt like it sometimes.

I parked a block from the school and hurried to the covered area where the younger kids played after the bell. Every day we surrendered our girls. How did we dare?

The play area was filled with a galloping, giggling mass, the children full of pent-up energy released, backpacks thrown to the ground. They looked so vulnerable, with their chapped-pink cheeks and raw hands.

Where were the girls?

In California, Amy with her fair coloring often stood out on the playground, but Boulder was the land of blondes, and she could get lost in the crowd. I looked for Erin's dark head. Half-blinded by rising anxiety, I worked through clusters of chatting parents as if needling through corduroy.

I was certain Gil had found us. He'd hunted us down and done what he'd sworn to do; he'd stolen my children away. All our efforts to begin again had only left us more vulnerable, trapped within our cocoon.

But here were my daughters, leaned up against the building, Erin in red tights under her school uniform, Amy in purple jeans.

The girls saw me and came forward. I moved toward them, locked on, searching for signs of anything wrong. But nothing was wrong. They looked like they always did at the end of a school day, Amy grubby and a little wild-eyed, Erin tidy and composed. And then my daughters and I were upon each other. I bent to give each a quick hug, trying, as usual, not to squeeze them too hard. But my relief couldn't stop me from imagining them as age-progressed milk-carton kids: two years older, five years, ten, the baby fat gone from their faces, their noses grown longer, their mouths wider, their jawlines more firm.

Driving out of California, Vinnie and I had decided we would not disguise ourselves in our new lives. He would not grow a beard. My long hair would remain brown. We wouldn't wear tinted contacts, gain or lose weight, speak with an accent, or learn to walk with a limp. Nor would we disguise the girls. We were giving them a new last name and moving them twelve hundred miles. That was trauma enough. But the fact remained that we'd taken them, just as their father had threatened to do.

Fourteen years Gil and I were together. He was, in spite of everything, family.

If I'd been the one to lose them, I'd scour the world. I'd devote every day of the rest of my life to finding my children, every dime and ounce of energy. And once they were safe again in my arms, I'd do whatever was necessary to make the person who'd taken them pay.

Would he?

12

In the Ecotone

Meanwhile, mountain lions came down from the hills.

Initially they kept to the outskirts of town, spotted on hiking trails or lingering near reservoirs, often guarding a fresh deer carcass or dragging it out of view; but soon there were sightings in more populated neighborhoods, places lions weren't expected to be, in driveways or crossing rivers and roads. Typically timid around humans, these mountain lions seemed different, curious and unafraid. They appeared during daylight hours, instead of at their usual feeding times, dawn and dusk, preying on the mule deer many residents welcomed. Boulder is a lushly planted urban environment, a small city surrounded by wilderness, with a history of preserving open space and encouraging wildlife. Though deer were often ruinous to gardens, they were part of nature and therefore, mostly, beloved.

Ecologists describe the place where distinct biological communities rub up against each other as an ecotone. In Greek, *eco* means "house," and *tone* means "tension." Overlapping communities "divide the house," creating instability, a chaos that can enrich biodiversity. The resulting adaptations and interactions are called edge effects. These are not solely benign. In an ecotone, dynamics can change between predator and prey.

By the time our family moved into the house on Tenth Street, lion sightings in Boulder had doubled from the previous year. Pets now began disappearing from homes in the canyons at an alarming rate: rabbits from hutches, cats and more cats, and dogs. A black Lab was found with its throat torn out, a German shepherd with its neck snapped and chest opened wide. But no one acted until a lion snatched a valuable red deer from a Coal Creek Canyon herd. The ranchers, who sold their pricey venison to local restaurants, hired a specialist, a cat hunter from the western slope. The hunter worked out the lion's habitual six-mile circuit, and his hounds tracked and treed it. Two men in the party shot the lion dead. An article in the *Daily Camera* cast doubt on their right to do so. Was this particular cat even responsible for the attacks?

The Division of Wildlife called an emergency neighborhood meeting up in Coal Creek. Some residents in attendance felt the lions were extremely dangerous and should be tagged and relocated or killed. Others felt that sporadic loss of livestock, or even a cherished pet, was the price of living in the canyon. The cats were by their nature harmless to people, they insisted. The Division of Wildlife, also inclined to this view, made a decision: Let the mountain lions be.

Over two months in the spring of 1990, eight more dogs were attacked and killed.

Michael Sanders, a resource specialist with Boulder County Parks and Open Space, had been recording sightings for months. He feared that pets had become a gateway drug for the lions. Interviewed in the *Denver Post*, he warned that humans might be next.

Vinnie and I never saw this reporting at the time. If it was a topic of local conversation, we remained unaware. Though our house sat only blocks from the foothills, we stayed away from the wilds. We did take the girls walking along Boulder Creek, but we weren't hikers or runners or cyclists.

We were, in a profound sense, an indoor family, the house on Tenth Street and its inhabitants comprising a distinct community of four. In hiding we preferred each other's company—it was safer that way. We weren't hermits; we had jobs, with bosses and clients who were willing for the time being to ask no questions and pay us under the table. The girls had made friends at school. We'd met, and liked, many of our neighbors. But our relationships remained necessarily superficial. We feared the chaos we'd surely unleashed when we ran from Gil. We feared complacency, and the consequences of brushing up against the world we'd left behind. And Gil. Above all, we feared Gil.

SPRING OF 1990, late afternoon. Vinnie at work, the girls still at school.

In our breakfast room at the back of the house, I hunched over my drafting table, painstakingly cutting up type and dropping in corrections to a brochure. The job was for our next-door neighbor, Jim, who ran a small ad agency—I'd promised him boards by the end of the day. And now someone was knocking on the front door. Can't be Jim, I thought. He knows to come through the yard.

An eight-point lowercase *p* floated at the tip of my X-Acto knife. I centered it over an error and pinned it with the blade, wiggled the *p* to line it up, and pressed it into place.

The knocking grew louder, more insistent.

I walked through the kitchen, into the hall and then the living room. The front part of the house was cool and dim, filled again with green light from the Virginia creeper.

The window in our front door framed a woman's face. I had an urge to turn heel and disappear back to the drafting table, but the woman had seen me. I heard her voice calling through the door, "Mrs. Palmer?"

I opened up reluctantly.

The woman eyed our nameplate. "Not Hirshberg? Right?"

"Right. Palmer."

The woman shifted her briefcase and held out her hand. I shook it. She stated her name, forgotten in an instant, but the next part came through loud and clear. The woman was a social worker. "I'm here from Sacred Heart School." When I flinched she added quickly, "Your children are fine. But I need to talk to you about Erin. May I come in?"

Stepping aside, it felt as if I were letting something treacherous into my home.

The social worker brought the outdoors in with her, cool air seeping from the fabric of her suit. She peered around our living room, taking in the books on the shelves, the toys on the floor, the remnants of breakfast on a table. She was saying something about Erin, Erin had done something, or said something. My ears roared. Oh, I thought, Erin *told*. Our names, maybe; maybe more; maybe everything. I imagined police and a courtroom, the girls taken away.

". . . has nothing to eat. Erin begs food from the other children."

Erin begs food? I laughed. I couldn't help it.

The social worker frowned.

"We give her money for hot lunch," I explained.

"That's not what she told me, Mrs. Palmer."

I heard Gil's voice in my head. *Feed your children.* "Erin has food!" I protested. "Maybe she lost her money. Or she's saving it." My voice rose. "Or some other kid is stealing from her. Did you even—"

"Please, Mrs. Palmer," the social worker interrupted. She gestured at the couch. "Why don't we sit?"

As if this were her house. But making a scene was unwise. I did as she asked.

"Your daughters seem well cared for," the social worker said soothingly.

Daughters? Had she also spoken to Amy?

"We have to look into these things, you understand," she said.

"I'll tell you what. School lets out in twenty minutes. Why don't you follow me back, and we'll meet in Erin's classroom. We can talk to her together."

I shook my head. "My husband has the car. He's picking them up."

"That would be . . . the stepfather? If he's doing pickup, that's even better. I'll drive you over. We'll all talk. It shouldn't take long to straighten this out. Or I can wait here with you until they get home."

I imagined the four of us trapped with the social worker. Vinnie would be blindsided. The girls would be scared. The social worker would misinterpret their fear. I had to get this woman out of our house.

"I'm in the middle of working," I said, "and my deadline is *now*." I heard how that sounded and segued into apology and appeasement. "I'm sorry about this. I can come to school tomorrow. What time is good for you?"

We set up an appointment. The social worker seemed mollified. I led her out to the porch but didn't breathe easier until she drove away.

I lowered onto the top step and, hugging my knees, looked anxiously to the end of the block. Soon our car turned onto our street. I saw Vinnie at the wheel, and in the back, the tops of the girls' heads, one dark, one fair.

Vinnie parked. They all climbed out and the girls ran to me. A quick embrace from Erin before she hurried inside. Amy, giggling, locked me into one of her patented tricky-tricky hugs. Impossible to free yourself and why would you want to? But then she abruptly let go and followed her sister.

Vinnie looked at me from the foot of the steps.

"What's happened," he said.

In my previous life I'd hated being watched, always certain I'd be found wanting. But there was never any threat in Vinnie's attention. As he stood there, I felt the workings of his lively, curious mind, and absorbed his scrutiny.

"I'll tell you later," I said.

Content to wait, he climbed the steps and sat beside me. He took my hand. Furniture stain darkened the tips of his nails. He scrubbed and scrubbed but could never get it all off. I didn't care, but it drove him crazy.

We watched our neighbors come home. Slam of car doors and the front doors of houses opening. Up the street a child climbed a tree. Someone whistled for a dog. Our elderly next-door neighbor came out onto his porch to collect his mail. He waved at us. We waved at him. We were just another family. We often wondered: Who else on this block was not who they seemed to be?

That night, while tucking Erin into bed, she asked me to turn off the light. Under cover of dark she confessed to spending her lunch money at recess on candy. She really, really wanted it. I saw her fishing change from her backpack, saw her gliding down a hallway, bangs in her eyes and coins in her fist, headed for the vending machines. She'd lied to the social worker because she didn't want to get in trouble. I knew that fear, a wretched thing hovering. Getting past it was a life's work.

"Are you mad at me?" she asked.

"I'm mad at myself. Did the lady pressure you?"

"She wanted to know what we have for *dinner*." Erin was fighting off tears. "Mommy, I didn't tell."

"I know, sweetheart."

The sudden conviction that she never would left me dizzy. What a position we'd put this child in.

"I'll talk to them tomorrow," I said. "I can fix it, don't worry. But you have to stop with the candy."

"I will."

"It's not good for you. You need to eat lunch."

"I'm sorry," she said, sniffling.

She had nothing to be sorry for. She was such a strong girl, loyal and brave. In her short life she'd been through so much. Why wouldn't she want something sweet?

THAT JUNE, TWO mountain lions treed a medical student in Sunshine Canyon. In July a lioness was seen in the parking lot of Boulder Community Hospital. Also in July, a man in a North Boulder subdivision videotaped two large cats that loitered on his hillside for hours. In August, higher into the foothills, a four-year-old boy and his father on the way to their outhouse encountered an inquisitive lion. The boy's father, who'd spotted the same animal the previous day, was carrying a gun. When the lion advanced, he felt he had to shoot.

I spoke to Mom not long after this incident, calling from my usual payphone outside Safeway; I was still afraid of using our house line. I didn't mention the lions—I didn't know about them. I did tell her about meeting with the social worker. She grew quiet, a silence I associated with disapproval. I thought it was because she still didn't know where we were. Recently, she'd suggested that all this secrecy might no longer be necessary. But it wasn't that. She had news. She'd returned from church on Sunday to find that someone had broken into her home. They'd emptied drawers onto the floor, along with the contents of her filing cabinet. They'd pulled books from the shelves. It took her a while to realize that her address book was the only thing missing. I pictured the fat volume that lived by the phone, its padded red cover and alphabetized entries, names and numbers crossed out as people moved or died.

Only one person in the world would have wanted it. And he wanted me to know.

I saw him roaming California, as he used to do, landing in Carlsbad to prey on my mom. He'd have checked her comings and goings, establishing her routine. He must've snuck through the mobile home park's security gate, likely on foot as a car entered or exited. Then he'd made his way. The streets at Lakeshore Gardens all looked alike, the homes confoundingly similar, but he knew where Mom lived. I tried to take consolation in the fact that he hadn't confronted her, seeking only some trace of where we'd run. Well, he could phone every number in her book, dial them forward and backward, and none would lead him to me.

"Did you call the police?" I asked.

"I did. An address book—they thought I was nuts."

"Change the locks."

"I'm not going to do that," she said. "I'm not afraid of him."

"Be extra careful, okay? Keep your eyes open?"

A gloomy laugh.

"I'm serious, Mom."

After we hung up, I thought about Gil's state of mind. Why *hadn't* he confronted Mom? And why, in all these months, hadn't he petitioned the court, trying to regain his parental rights by throwing himself on their mercy? He could have sworn he'd reformed, or said he'd found religion, or assured them he'd now be a model divorced dad. Mom would have gotten word of this eventually and passed it on to me. Instead, he preferred to stalk us. He wanted us—he wanted me—scared.

AWAKENED FROM A dead sleep, I sat straight up in bed. Vinnie stood at an open window.

"What?" I said.

"Come look," he said.

I climbed out and joined him.

Below us, in the side yard, a uniformed officer stood at the gate. The cop was shining a flashlight over the top, into our back yard. A radio crackled. Someone said, "Block's been cordoned off."

Filled with dread, I asked Vinnie, "Is it Gil?"

"I don't think so." He called down softly, "The gate isn't locked. You can go in."

The cop spoke without looking up. "Noooo, not going to do that. You've got a mountain lion back there."

Vinnie and I went into the hallway. A door on the western side of the house led out to a derelict balcony. Vinnie unlocked it. Our back yard was lit like a stage. Trees and bushes looked like actors, fallen red apples like props scattered in the tall grass. A light breeze set everything to trembling.

"There it is," Vinnie said.

Halfway up our Chinese elm, a mountain lion lolled on a branch. The animal emanated a barely restrained power you'd hope never to witness unleashed. Its tail switched insouciantly.

I slipped beneath Vinnie's arm.

A man in safari gear entered the yard from the alley. He gripped in one hand some sort of long-barreled weapon.

"Dart gun," Vinnie murmured.

The hunter had become the hunted.

This lion, I later learned, was first spotted four blocks away on The Hill, in the small commercial area that served the west end of the university. That night hundreds of students had crowded the streets, many drunkenly celebrating their return from summer break. Near midnight someone called the police to report a lion watching from the shadows. The animal was only doing what came naturally, the change in its behavior precipitated by humans, who'd altered the terms of engagement. The police called Wildlife Management before tracking the lion into our yard.

The following year, a lion would kill Scott Lancaster, an eighteen-year-old high school senior, not in Boulder but forty miles southwest, in Idaho Springs. Scott would go out for a run during his free period and never return. Searchers would find his body on a rocky slope powdered with snow, his face peeled back, an enormous hole in his chest. His heart had been removed. At first, law enforcement believed Lancaster's death was the work of a vicious human killer, but while inspecting the crime scene they noticed a lion sitting in a juniper grove, watching them. When the cat slinked away, they gave chase. A sniper felled the animal from two hundred yards.

Investigators speculated that this lion, an adult male, might have been one of those sighted in Boulder the previous summer.

Our lion was female.

Two cops flanked the man in the safari suit. One carried a drawn pistol, the other a shotgun. Cautiously, they all approached the elm. The man in the safari outfit sat down on the grass. He bent his legs and braced his knees. He lifted the dart gun to his lips, aimed, and took his shot. A muffled *thwap*. The lion, hit in the thigh, recoiled and scrambled upward, climbing higher into the tree. Another dart flew.

The cat's body loosened visibly—she was already woozy. Her head swiveled, the fur at her neck a liquid rippling. She was looking at us, at Vinnie and me. My stomach dropped. The lioness's eyes glittered like mirrored emeralds. I'd never seen anything so beautiful, so terrifying.

13

Imposters

Colorado, New Mexico, Arizona, California. We left in the middle of the night and drove straight through, stopping only for gas and meals. The girls were mostly knocked out, and Vinnie slept whenever I took the wheel, but I dozed fitfully, kept awake by the dramatic descent from snow-covered peaks, and by hours of desert, the morning sun at our backs, the setting sun blinding. We were retracing—in reverse—the route we'd taken when we'd fled. It felt like time-travel.

We arrived at Lakeshore Gardens late evening on the second day. Visiting Mom a month after Gil's break-in probably wasn't smart, but it was because of the break-in that I had to see her.

Vinnie and I had another reason to visit Carlsbad: we still needed ID.

We'd put off this last step in establishing our new identities for more than a year, out of fear of being caught, and also because we were stuck in a classic catch-22 situation: Social Security required a government-issued photo to complete an adult application, while Colorado's DMV required a Social Security number to get a photo ID. Then I'd discovered that in California it was still possible to apply for a driver's license with only a birth certificate and a utility bill to prove residence. We already had our forged certificates; the plan now was to borrow (with permission, of course) an electric bill from Esther, Mom's neighbor and best friend at Lakeshore Gardens, and doctor it up.

Pulling up to the park's front gate I scanned the street, looking for Gil. I saw no cars parked nearby, and no pedestrians. Vinnie punched in the code and we entered.

"I *think* I remember this place," Erin said, as if it had been years.

I directed Vinnie to park in Esther's driveway. He pulled in as far as possible, to hide the California plate we'd never replaced. Then the girls were out of the car, running to greet Mom, who must've seen us from her front porch and was walking over. At the sight of her, happiness surged through me, followed by melancholy and guilt. I'd deprived Mom of her grandchildren, deprived her of family. If Gil ever turned up again, she'd be forced to deal with him alone.

I checked out houses along the street. All presented blank faces. Mom saw, and her lips thinned in disapproval. More time-travel: I was again sixteen.

She turned to Erin and Amy. Held each girl at arm's length and exclaimed over how much she'd grown. My daughters glowed.

Vinnie came forward and hugged Mom.

"How was the drive?" she asked him.

"Good, long," he said. "Kind of weird. We're glad to be here."

Enough of this, I thought, knees weakening. I rushed Mom, and we fell into each other's arms. She held me up, or I held her up, or maybe we kept each other from falling. When we finally let go, I took a good long look at her. Over the past year she'd grown heavy. Her face was puffy, the bags under her eyes pronounced. Her thick hair, dyed blonde since I was a child, was now iron gray. She still wore it no-nonsense short, styled with water and a pocket comb.

"You look good," I said.

"Liar."

"I like the hair."

"I see yours got longer," she said.

And here came Esther down her drive: tiny, crippled with arthritis, smiling hard and blinking like an owl. I threw an arm around her shoulder and kissed her cheek.

Looking at Mom, I asked Esther, "So, do I look different?"

"No," Esther said.

"Mom," I said. "Mom? Do I *seem* different?"

She tilted her head, considering. "Different from what, Kerry-girl," she sighed, "and how would I know?"

I'D TOLD MOM we could only stay a few days, but when I reminded her, she acted as if it were news; she thought we'd be with her longer. I didn't know what to say. We'd pulled the girls out of school and purposely traveled midweek, just to be safe. We'd made appointments at different DMVs and our business would be conducted over two days. Both before and after, I hoped to keep away from Mom's house, the five of us busy with various beach-town outings. She agreed to this reluctantly, visibly displeased.

Vinnie went first at the DMV; I went second. Both offices were deserted, contrasting with every previous experience I'd ever had. The clerks accepted our forged birth certificates along with a copy of Esther's utility bill, altered to be in our names. While they went off to make copies, we stood there feeling conspicuous, but the clerks returned to the window unfazed. They absorbed our nervous babble about being uprooted New Yorkers who'd never needed to drive. We took written tests, and road tests. We got in line for photos. It was done. After suffering so much in advance—we'd prepared an expanding defense, in case of challenge—it should have been more harrowing.

Our last night, while settling in to watch TV with the girls after an early dinner, Mom sprang an alternate plan.

"There's a party over at the clubhouse," she said.

It was, apparently, someone's birthday.

"Oh," I said. "You want to go?"

"I want *you* to go, Kerry. I want you all to go."

"No, Mom. Why would we do that?"

"For me," she said. "You'd do it for me."

I couldn't say no.

We stopped by Esther's to pick her up, then we all walked to the clubhouse. The place was hopping, fifty or more retirees dressed in a mix of tracksuits and sparkles, talking and laughing and drinking and eating. Lights shined bright, the air was stuffy, the music loud. Sinatra, Nat King Cole, Dean Martin. The birthday girl, a behatted old-school dame named Maggie, guarded a multitiered cake from her wheelchair.

Mom took us over to say hello. We wished Maggie happy birthday, then Mom linked her arm in mine. "Let's make the rounds."

I'd met many of these people before.

"You remember my Kerry," Mom said again and again. "And her husband." She didn't name Vinnie. "These two little beauties are my granddaughters."

After a while, the little beauties got antsy and ran off, looking for food, Mom following.

A dapper gent standing near us asked Vinnie, "So how's business? Still selling lithographs?"

That the gent had remembered this factoid about Gil surprised me. On the other hand, he'd misidentified Vinnie, who aside from his height, looked nothing like Gil.

Vinnie said smoothly, "Yeah, but I've moved to a different gallery."

"Life of a salesman." The gent cleared his throat. "So. If I was looking to invest, who do you like?"

Vinnie furrowed his brow. He ran a hand through his hair. His stance shifted, his feet now set more widely apart. "Art deco," he said confidently. "Can't go wrong with Erté. Those prints really *move*."

His voice—was there more New York in it?

What was he *doing*?

Unnerved, I excused myself and went to get us cups of champagne punch. I swallowed most of mine at the serving table, and it went right to my head. I refilled my cup before heading back.

A lady with a long white braid had joined the dapper gent and was looking up at Vinnie in admiration. Well, there was much to admire. He was young (comparatively!) and vigorous and handsome. This lady I remembered as someone who often referred to Mom, incorrectly and amazingly, as "the gay divorcée." Sometimes the two of them met at the pool for a swim. They liked to make fun of the men, who tended to commandeer the facility, their preening breast strokes and competitive crawls emptying the pool of women, driving them to lounge chairs and brutal observation.

The lady with the braid said to Vinnie, "You know, my son and his wife live up in Marin County. You all should get together. What town are you in again?"

Mom had worked her way back around to join us, Esther in tow. "Kentfield," Mom said. Which was where the girls and I had lived two years ago, with Gil.

"A lovely town," Esther said, grinning puckishly.

"I told you, Carol," Mom said. "Give him their number, why don't you."

I stared at Mom. What the hell? What had she told this woman?

Why had she made us come here? She knew we were still in peril—my God, Gil had only just broken into her house—but she cared more about proving to her friends I still visited her. She was unreliable. I was unreliable, too. I'd risked my daughters' safety coming to this party because I felt guilty. It made me furious. I moved Erin closer and draped my forearms over her shoulders. She rested the back of her head on my chest.

Amy tugged on Vinnie's shirt, saying, "Vinnie." He picked her up, and she said, "Vinnie. Vinnie."

No one seemed to notice. No one pays attention to little girls.

The music surged, wild horns and a driving drumbeat, the opening to "Sing, Sing, Sing." Vinnie bent down so Carol could hear whatever he was saying. When he straightened, he caught my eye. He *twinkled*.

Jesus Christ. He was having fun.

ON THE WAY back to Mom's, Vinnie said, "What's wrong?" We had Amy between us, each holding a hand, while Mom and Esther and Erin walked ahead. The sun sat low in the sky, the last light like freshly washed oranges in a blue bowl.

I was, I realized, more than a little drunk.

"Who are you?" I said.

"What do you mean? I'm me."

"No. Who are you *now*?"

He swung Amy's arm and she giggled, swinging mine.

"I'm always me," Vinnie said.

"All we do is lie," I said. "Doesn't it bother you?"

"What? Back there?" He meant the clubhouse. "They wanted your husband so that's what I gave them. It was harmless, Kerry."

Maybe, I thought. Probably.

In *De Mendacio*, Saint Augustine defines a lie as "a statement at variance with the mind." The most grievous of these are lies that harm others while helping no one, followed by lies that harm but are meant to give aid. Then there are lies meant to amuse. Tonight, that was Vinnie.

"You were pretty convincing," I said. "I almost bought it."

"That's acting," he said.

It was what he'd once thought he would do: act. In his twenties, he'd loved the shape-shifting, how it felt like being a spy, 007 on stage. The key, he'd told me, was using your body to *imply*. You change superficial details while maintaining the core of who you are. Assuming, that is, that you know who you are.

"Why do you think they believed you?" I asked.

"Who knows? It was a nice group. Polite. And it was a party. These are older people, and I'd guess they don't like commotion. They have other things to worry about. I'm sure some of them don't see or hear all that well . . . but it's not like we were hurting anyone."

"Not tonight."

"You aren't serious."

"We're *imposters*."

Vinnie laughed. "Not exactly."

Most famous imposters, the ones they make movies about, are motivated by greed. They also seem addicted to the idea of getting away with something. Some, I supposed, were driven by fear or necessity—that would be us—while others attempted to heal old wounds through a new identity. Imposters dealt with a lack of goodness in themselves by exploiting the goodness in others, I realized suddenly. Or was I overdramatizing?

My head spun. It was too much.

A breeze had kicked up. The air smelled of the sea. The light fell, and a few leaves in the street moved alongside us; they looked like creatures scurrying. As if we'd choreographed it, Vinnie and I lifted Amy and swung her between us, higher and higher. Her laughter sounded like bells. Mom and Erin turned to look, Erin's expression impatient. She undoubtedly wanted to get back to her Nancy Drew novel; she'd been obsessed with the teenage investigator all year. But I couldn't read Mom. I fixated on the red tip of her burning cigarette—she'd never give up the coffin nails. It was aggravating, and worrying.

Ah, but her face. A raised eyebrow. A faint gleam to her forehead and cheeks. A slick of coral lipstick, a shade she'd worn forever.

I loved her, and I knew she loved me.

"Higher!" Amy cried. We swung her higher. I wanted to believe she believed she was flying.

IN THE GUEST room, where the girls slept, Mom sat on the bed between them, reading aloud from *The Mystery at Lilac Inn*. It brought back memories of her reading to me, so I sat on the floor and listened. But this was our last night, and it occurred to me Mom might want to spend time alone with Erin and Amy, so I got up and went into the hall, where I could still hear her voice. It made for a kind of duet with the voices from her living-room TV: Vinnie was watching the ten o'clock news. I couldn't see him, but I liked thinking about him comfortably ensconced in Mom's blue easy chair.

I studied two framed photos hung on the wall.

The first had been taken in Albuquerque, New Mexico, on Mom and Daddy's wedding day. Here was Daddy, guiding his bride into the passenger side of a 1940s sedan. Mom, dressed in a crisply tailored white suit and black pumps, had her head turned to greet the camera. Her smile was perfect, not posed but genuine. Daddy, clasping Mom's hand, had eyes only for her.

When my father went off to war in 1942, Mom was still a kid in high school, a basketball in one hand and a book in the other. By the time he returned, she'd transformed into a Wall Street secretary in a fitted wool suit, five foot two, eyes of blue, thick blonde hair curling around her shoulders. At McGlade's, in Columbus Circle, they eyed each other down the bar. Raymond, tall and thin, Black Irish, with dark hair and blue eyes. Mom used to say he wore his Air Force uniform like a tux. Flyboy, she'd thought disdainfully. That night, he'd come in with his best friend, Frank, also a veteran. The two men huddled on either side of a sailor who was saying loudly that he was gonna kill that sonofabitch Frankie, because Frankie had stolen the sailor's wife, Sal. But the sailor didn't know Frank from Mussolini. So Daddy threw an arm around his shoulder and confessed: *He* was Frankie, *he* was the thief. The sailor's face crimsoned with rage. And my father asked the one question that could change any conversation. *Where were you?* Meaning the war. And that was the end of that. Grinning, Daddy had locked eyes with Mom as he spoke. Two weeks later, she broke off her engagement to a naval officer.

Each workday evening, they met at the West 79th Street subway station after work, Mom running to Daddy's silhouette at the top of the stairs. Up and up, clobbered. Her heart. It's possible, she once told me, to die of love.

I turned my attention to the second photo, a black-and-white portrait of me at age four taken by my parents' friend, Joe Rosenthal, who was famous for the image of American soldiers planting the flag at Iwo Jima. In this photo, I stood next to an old RCA television and a ghostly game of football. I wore one of Mom's dresses, a linen sheath, and a little black hat with a veil. The dress fell to my ankles. With one hand I lifted the fabric carefully up from the hips to reveal my Mom's high-heeled alligator slingbacks. What a thrill.

And now here was Mom. She draped an arm over my shoulder and knocked her head gently against mine. "When are you coming back, honey?"

To my shame, I acted as if it might be soon; I even implied we might return to California permanently. I didn't mean to give her false hope—I lied to avoid her criticism. I lied to avoid an argument. I lied to be loved.

"Why don't you take the photos back with you?"

This should've pleased me. I wanted them. But I wanted more for her to want them, so I said no.

"You keep them." I tipped my chin at four-year-old Kerry. "This way you won't forget me."

SOME WEEKS LATER a package from California arrived in Boulder, the box left on our porch by the mailbox beside the front door. It was addressed to "Kerry and Vinnie," no last names, in what I took to be Esther's spidery hand.

The box held two lacy, flouncy, flowery dresses that sprang open like Jack-in-the-boxes when freed. One was pink, the other lavender. They were not Mom's style, nor mine, nor the girls', though they'd be delighted to have fancy new clothes. I set the dresses aside.

Resting at the bottom of the box were two manilla envelopes, one large, the other letter-sized. I opened the larger envelope first and slid out two framed photos: me wearing Mom's dress, and the shot of her and Daddy on their wedding day.

I knew the perfect place for the wedding photo; I'd hang it beside a pastel drawing I'd done of Vinnie and me jumping off a bridge holding hands. I studied the Rosenthal portrait, touched a fingertip to my little-girl cheek. I'd have to think about this one. Maybe I'd hang it by the front door. I liked the idea of the child I once was standing guard over who I'd become.

I opened the smaller envelope. It contained our new California driver's licenses. As per usual with the DMV, the photos did not flatter. They were also undeniably Vinnie and me.

Mom had tucked in a short note.

You have what you need now, Kerry. Don't put it off. Take care of this right away.

Again, Vinnie went first. In the parking lot of the Boulder Social Security office, he sat in the car for more than an hour, staring at the building's front windows while trying to land on a plausible story as to why a grown man nearing forty did not have a tax identification number. His mind fizzed with fear. Were there security guards inside? He was sweating, his shirt stuck to his back. Flop sweat, he thought.

Use the fear, he told himself, and climbed out of the car.

He clutched his documents and got in line and fidgeted. He said loudly, to no one in particular, "Ants in my pants." Without turning, the woman ahead of him moved away.

At the counter Vinnie lowered his gaze. "I'm, I'm . . . scared," he said haltingly. "I'm scared I'm going to be in trouble."

"What do you mean?" the clerk said.

Vinnie laid his documents down. "My boss said I have to show you this."

The clerk looked at his birth certificate and the driver's license from California and asked, "Have you moved here?"

Vinnie nodded.

"Did you lose your card?"

"My boss said I need a number for taxes. Before, I always got cash."

"You've never had a card?"

Vinnie said desperately, "I need a number."

"Okay," the clerk said.

Vinnie looked up then. The clerk was smiling. Tears sprang to Vinnie's eyes. He wasn't acting now. The clerk reached over, patted his hand, and said, "I'll help you fill out the form."

Two weeks later, it was my turn.

When the clerk asked why I'd never had a number, I said I'd been a kept woman. I said my boyfriend was rich, we'd lived together since I was a teenager, and he'd paid for everything. I'd never worked, I'd never had to work. We broke up, though. And now I needed a job.

I was jabbering—I clamped my mouth shut.

The clerk looked bored.

An irrational burst of anger coursed through me. I was an imposter. Couldn't she see?

The clerk passed me the application form. "Bring it back to this window after you've filled everything in."

"I don't know what happened," I said.

She passed me a pen.

Goddamn it—I'd never escape my own lies.

"Listen, *listen*," I said. "It was like he owned me."

14

Names of the Dead

Four years passed with no further sign of Gil. I finally told Mom where we'd run, and Vinnie told his parents. The summer of 1994 we drove to Florida to see them. Earlier that year, they'd both been diagnosed with late-stage bowel cancer. Both had undergone colectomies. Their prognoses were fuzzy. But they remained in good spirits throughout the visit, kind and welcoming. How easily they might have rejected the girls and me for keeping Vinnie from them.

My mother-in-law, who was a sensitive soul, saw my worries and pulled me aside. "Your daughters," she said, eyes shining, "they're so bright, so loving. They're wonderful girls. We adore them."

They were wonderful girls. For five years now I'd watched them closely for signs of trouble, but they seemed to have weathered our disappearance—"seemed" being a matter of interpretation. How do you separate growing pains from trauma? How much will a child hide from a parent, no matter how hard you look? Amy, at eight, had charisma. She was comfortable with adults. She'd been bullied, though, at Sacred Heart, so after two years we'd moved her to our neighborhood public school. The bullying continued, the reasons for it, despite numerous parent-teacher conferences, elusive. Still, she seemed okay. Erin, soon to turn thirteen, was harder to read, newly secretive and gently defiant. The storms of adolescence were brewing.

My mother-in-law smiled. "We adore you, too, you know. For yourself, but especially because you make our son happy."

This brought tears to my eyes. I loved my in-laws as well, not only because they were Vinnie's parents, but because they were themselves.

They lived in a mobile home park, just like Mom, but Florida felt like another country, the air thick with humidity, the grass indestructible, the greenery shocking in its intensity. Everywhere I looked I saw cabbage palms and mangroves and banana trees. Succulent-looking flowers hummed with bees. We walked on the beach and swam in the bathwater-warm Atlantic, went home and swam in the park's pool, water striders zipping by as if on water skis. I played the piano in the community clubhouse. My father-in-law played chess with Vinnie and checkers with Amy. My mother-in-law cooked with Erin. We ate and talked and stayed up late and talked and ate. We sweated in the sub-tropical heat. And I saw exactly where Vinnie came by his love of food and dancing, his gentleness, his curiosity.

On our last night, after dinner we moved into the den to watch TV and found whatever program we'd had in mind preempted by news: In Los Angeles, O. J. Simpson, charged with the murders of his ex-wife, Nicole Brown Simpson, and her friend Ron Goldman, rolled slowly down a freeway in a white Bronco, police cars in low-speed pursuit. Few details about the murders were public knowledge, but what was known had a familiar ring: a charismatic and jealous ex-husband, a former wife determined to get away. Did Vinnie's parents see the parallel to our situation? We didn't discuss that, partly because of the girls, but also because farewells were on everyone's mind.

The next morning, driving west on I-10, hours of rain matched our somber mood. In Mobile, Alabama, on a whim we detoured to New Orleans. Approaching the French Quarter, while stopped at a light, a street sign changed direction in the wind. This, I thought, was one of those places where you might lose your mind, your way, your heart. Iron lace, jazz heard through open doorways, a voodoo museum. We bought the girls masks and beads and, hiding from the brutal sun, downed beignets at a café. Across the street a priest strolled in front of the cathedral, black cassock swinging. I licked powdered sugar from my fingers, took out my notebook, and jotted down a few words. I imagined the priest was me, but also, of course, not-me. Where had he come from? What was he thinking? What sort of trouble was he in? My pulse quickened—how I longed to be creative. There was room for that now in my life. I made another note, and another. And in this way, *All Saints*, a novel about three lonely people who cross paths in 1950s New Orleans, was born.

On the way out of town we stopped at a service station, and while Vinnie filled the tank, I called Mom. I anticipated the usual catch-up: I'd tell her about our visit with Vinnie's parents; she'd feed me gossip and her bridge scores.

Instead, she told me that my former stepdaughter had called; Gil had been arrested in New York for murder and convicted at trial. He was serving his sentence at a prison in upstate New York.

Horrified, I asked Mom who he'd killed. She didn't know. I pictured a stranger in a bar. I pictured a man who'd double-crossed him. I pictured a faithless girlfriend.

"The important thing is you're safe," she said. "Your family's safe."

My chest squeezed.

"I'm having surgery tomorrow, Kerry," she added. "It's the goddamn veins."

OVER THE PAST couple of years, Mom had had two procedures to address her peripheral vascular disease: angioplasties on both legs—slices from ankle to groin and the clogged veins stripped away—and what she called a "Roto-Rooter job," an operation to scour out the plaque blocking 90 percent of her carotid arteries. This blockage was discovered by way of a dream, Mom awakening one night from the malevolent company of whispering birds to an earthquake. Like any sensible Californian, she got out of bed and moved into a doorway to wait out the shaking. The walls flexed; the floor rolled. When it was over, she threw on a bathrobe and went out into the street. She expected to see her neighbors streaming from their homes, but the street sat empty. All lights were out. She couldn't understand it. She went home and climbed into bed. In the morning she consulted the newspaper; there'd been no earthquake. A quick trip to the doctor revealed that she'd probably experienced a transient ischemic attack, her brain, deprived of oxygen, tricking itself.

I flew to California to help her recover from that operation. While a nurse changed the bandages on both sides of Mom's neck, I inspected the jagged scars. "All you need are bolts," I said.

In her hospital bed, she'd barked out a laugh, certain she was home free.

And then, while we were in Florida, her renal veins had collapsed. The doctors scheduled more surgery. When I told her I'd get on a plane, she said, "Don't bother, honey. It's just more of the same. Esther will help."

Within a few weeks, her renal veins again failed. Due to a fifty-year two-pack-a-day smoking habit, she was not a candidate for a kidney transplant. The doctors decided to put in a stent.

I traveled to Carlsbad to see her through the operation. When it failed, Mom was put on dialysis.

For a month I drove her to a center in San Diego for thrice-weekly treatments. One day, while on our way home, she announced that she was "done." At the age of sixty-nine she was "pulling the plug."

I steered to the side of the road and killed the engine. "You can't do that, Mom."

To which she replied, "I most certainly can. Dialysis is unnatural. I feel like I'm being embalmed."

"That's crazy. They're not putting anything in you that isn't yours."

"I know that," she said sharply. "I'm telling you, it makes me feel like I'm already dead."

"Oh my God, that's awful. Why would you say that? What do you mean?"

I'm ashamed now to admit that my thoughts were all for myself, less anticipation of loss than a demoralizing fear: Would Mom's death be my fault? My mother had had her share of unhappiness, but her life in recent years had been safe and secure. She loved her home at the beach. She had things to do and many friends. She had *me*. But when I'd suggested she come and live with us in Colorado, she refused. Maybe, I thought darkly, the twists and turns of my life had asked too much of her. Maybe she believed I should have found another way.

As if reading my mind, she said, "It's got nothing to do with you, Kerry. I'm tired, that's all. I'm ready. And kidney failure's not a bad way to go."

She'd long kept a typewritten list of the dead, people she prayed for. There were 224 names on this list, including her brother, Warren, who'd fallen down an elevator shaft at age seven, her brothers Willie and Leo, and her sister Evelyn. It included my grandmother, who'd died in an old-age home in upstate New York, but not my grandfather, who ran away with another woman during the Great Depression. Daddy, of course, was there at the top. All recent additions Mom had written by hand. The final entry was dated May 1994. By August, she herself was gone.

HER LAST DAYS are seared into memory. Helping her bathe, telling her to hold a washcloth over her eyes while I rinsed her hair, as if she were my child. I cooked her a fried egg in butter, and when she took a bite, she trembled. She gripped my hands.

"You are my girl forever. You're the only one who understands."

People cried at the wake, including Vinnie. Erin and Amy pressed in close to him, seeking comfort. How lucky we were to have him. Amy had recently asked Erin: *Why do we call Vinnie by his name?* Astonishing that after all this time she didn't understand he was her stepfather, that she had another dad. More astonishing still that she and Erin had never talked about it. So Vinnie took Amy out for a walk and explained what we'd done and why. She took it calmly, said she *liked* calling him Vinnie. It made her feel special.

My Uncle Vincent, who'd been sitting at the back of the viewing room, approached Mom's casket. He stood beside me and bowed his head. When he finished his prayer, he glared down at Mom.

She didn't look like herself. They'd gotten her hairstyle wrong, and her neck bulged distressingly, though they'd disguised the scars from the Roto-Rooter job. The dress I'd picked for her to be buried in was crinkly blue cotton, bits of shiny metal embedded in the fabric like stars. The square neckline showed off her handsome collarbones.

Confrontationally, as if she might sit up and argue, my uncle said, "You should've waited, kid." He reached for my hand—I'll always be grateful for that—and scolded his little sister. "Dorothy, I wish you'd done the right thing."

By her lights she had. My mother knew who she was. I was glad she'd eluded being told otherwise.

IN HER FILE cabinet, I found a note: *Kerry, if you want to search for your birth mother, her name is Katherine Kleinsmark.*

This information was both a gift and a blow.

Where had she learned my birth mother's name, and when? Why had she never told me? Anger flashed through me, followed by hope, then despair. Who had she been protecting? By what right? I got out Mom's list of the dead and scanned it, relieved that Katherine Kleinsmark's name wasn't there. Though how would she have known?

Did I even want to find my birth mother? I wasn't sure. I'd just lost the only mom I'd ever known and couldn't wrap my mind around this. Many years later, when I finally searched for both my birth mother and my son, it sadly came to nothing. A bitter disappointment. But I knew how lucky I was in love, how lucky in family.

IN 1996, AFTER *All Saints* was accepted for publication, I flew to New York to meet with my agent and editor. Afterward, instead of returning to my hotel, I rode the subway downtown to the criminal courthouse. I wanted to see what could be learned about Gil's conviction. With the help of a patient clerk, I discovered that either Mom or Gil's daughter had gotten significant parts of the story wrong.

In the early morning hours of August 1, 1993, a white male had fired several gunshots through a window into a bar at the corner of Eighty-third Street and York Avenue. No one was killed, or even hit.

It was a relief that Gil hadn't murdered anyone, but my emotions roiled, because the story I'd believed supported our decision to run. Now I wondered what really happened.

Immediately after the shooting, I read, two bouncers ran into the street. They followed the armed culprit a short distance before he turned around and fired at them. A hot dog vendor working his stand described the gunman to police as "an older man who carried a cane." He pointed out the building the man had entered. The vendor believed the gunman was on the third floor.

The officers entered the building from the street and ascended the stairs. On the second floor they walked through a vacant apartment before exiting through a window out onto the fire escape. They noted on the windowsill above them an ashtray that held a lit cigarette. The officers drew their guns. They shined flashlights into the darkened apartment, onto a man in boxer shorts lying prone on the floor, one arm concealed under a quilt; a cane had been slung over a doorknob. One of the officers called out. No answer. After a second callout, the man responded. The officer climbed in through the window. He withdrew the man's hand from under the quilt but found no gun, though police later recovered a .45 caliber pistol above a closet's door jamb.

Gil, identified at the scene by the bouncers, was charged with two counts of attempted murder, reckless endangerment, and criminal possession of a weapon in the second and third degrees. Upon questioning, he admitted to being a heavy drinker, but stated he'd been awakened by noise from the bar. He'd loaded his gun with a full clip to "take care of things." Outside the bar, he'd fired a single shot in the air before aiming through the front window.

In the end, he took a plea bargain: dismissal of the attempted murder and reckless endangerment charges in exchange for admission of guilt on two charges of illegal gun possession. The judge sentenced him to concurrent terms of two to six years.

I stared in disbelief and horror at the name of the prison upstate where he'd been remanded: Cape Vincent Correctional. Cape *Vincent*? What were the odds? Gil was forced to see Vinnie's name daily—I could only imagine how it made him feel.

The clerk then said he'd been released on parole.

He was *out*? I shivered. My gut told me he was here in the city, living again at his mother's apartment.

I took the subway to the Upper East Side, exited at Eighty-sixth Street, and walked toward York Avenue. A reckless mission, but I felt compelled. Eight years ago I'd disappeared, and so in a sense had Gil. I wanted to see who he was now, and I wanted him to see me. The closer I got, the faster I walked. The faster I walked, the harder it was to breathe.

There. There was his building, redbrick and iron, with a small street-level business beneath four residential floors.

The outer door was unlocked. In the tiny tiled vestibule I faced a bank of ten mailboxes. There was no name for Apartment 3B, and no buzzer. Was he in there or not? I agonized, then set off up the stairs.

The exterior door opened and a man blundered through. I turned to face him, my heart hammering.

The man stared up at me. Frozen on the step, I stared down at him. I felt . . .*treed*. Like that lioness trapped in our Boulder back yard.

Who was the predator here, who the prey?

The man wasn't Gil, of course. He couldn't be—Gil didn't live here. He'd spent half a decade in prison, and his mother had died years earlier. There'd been no one to hang on to her flat.

The man pushed past me.

I stumbled outside. And I said aloud, over and over, *Let it be, let it go. Let it be.*

15

Elements

In 1999 the US House of Representatives impeached President Bill Clinton. In 2000, with *Bush v. Gore,* we lost one of our last, best chances to address climate change. On September 11, 2001, a terrorist attack on the World Trade Center in New York changed not just the city but the entire world.

For our family, though, as for millions of others, day-to-day life remained substantially the same. We worked. The girls went to school. By now our false identities had gone unquestioned for a decade, and fears about Gil had eased. We did not feel entirely safe, but the dangers had changed. Gil became in these years a kind of void, like a lunar eclipse. You couldn't look directly at him without going blind.

This both connected and separated me from my girls.

They never asked questions about Gil. They never wanted to talk about him. Their lack of curiosity confused me, especially as they grew older, but it also suited: I wanted them to forget not only what he'd done but my part in it: how I'd stayed in the marriage too long; how I'd allowed him to terrorize me; how I'd failed, catastrophically, to manage him and protect us, until there was no longer a choice and we disappeared. Since running, Vinnie and I had given Erin and Amy two loving parents. We'd created an alternate sun, the girls circling us like planets throughout their childhoods. But the void of Gil's absence remained.

Shadows were inevitable. They fell more on one child than the other.

Erin struggled in middle and high school, plagued, as teenagers can be, by hormones, and ungovernable emotions, and the urge to take risks. She shoplifted, she drank, she ran wild. She was hard to get along with, touchy and volatile. She was sometimes mean. This all felt normal to me, more or less, her teenage life unfolding largely out of sight, as it does for everyone. I did not want to control her, but she needed control. This could not come from Vinnie. I loved Erin and I knew she loved me. We fought things out alone, me often in furious pursuit, she slamming the door in my face. She was a good student, which reassured us, though I think now I was too willing to be reassured—in any case, it weakened any challenge. She could always trot out her report card as proof she was fine. But she wasn't fine.

Adolescents spend so much time feeling, acting out who they think they are and who they might become. What did it mean to Erin that we'd vanished? What did it mean that we'd changed her identity? How much did this contribute to her troubles? And what did she feel about Gil? Did she secretly wish we could all be together again?

When I asked if she remembered living in Kentfield, in the one-bedroom apartment on Sir Francis Drake Boulevard, she said she mostly did not, though she did recall sitting stone-still under the glass-topped kitchen table while an argument—the arguers unnamed—raged above her. I asked what she remembered about Santa Cruz. The question made her wary. Her recollections of that year were patchy and anodyne. She remembered her daily walk to Gault Elementary School. She remembered her bed shoved up next to Amy's in their small room. She remembered trips to the board-walk, and the two of them home sick with chicken pox.

Occasionally, she talked about visiting Grandma in Carlsbad while Gil had Amy. I pressed her, trying to work out what he meant to her, but whatever I said angered Erin, and she stormed away to her room.

The void.

Her father. *Her father.*

In 1999 she graduated from high school and went off to college back east. The house felt empty without her, but it was also peaceful, a relief. When she returned home that Thanksgiving—and for every visit thereafter—she was again the child she'd once been: thoughtful, friendly, kind, a magical transformation known to parents everywhere, separation being the catalyst for change. She seemed to have made it through. She spent her junior year in Santiago, Chile, where students on campus cheered 9/11. Her thesis on intergenerational trauma in young Chileans who hadn't lived through the terrors of Pinochet exhibited an eerie if distant relevance to someone with her history.

Amy, on the other hand, could not be probed for memories of her father because she had none. What did the void mean to her?

She watched her sister's teenage rebellion, and took notes. Her weapon would be willful charm. And indeed, she was a delight. Deceptions and minor falls from grace went unnoticed, or unacknowledged. If she was hurting, she hid it well. She was scary smart but underachieving, adored by teachers who gave her Ds. By the time she was a junior in high school, she itched to drop out. Maddened, I'd threaten, only half-jokingly, that this would happen over my dead body.

She did it anyway. I didn't fight her. And I lived.

THE SUMMER OF 2002, the Rocky Mountains went up in flames.

The Hayman Fire was the largest in state history, its record unchallenged for the next eighteen years. Roughly 138,000 acres burned over 24 days; 133 homes were destroyed and 5,340 people evacuated; the smoke, visible up and down the Front Range, featured a plume so massive it made its own weather. Fatalities included a woman who suffered a fatal asthma attack from smoke inhalation, and five firefighters enroute from Oregon who died from injuries sustained in a traffic accident.

On Saturday, June 8, at 9:15 a.m., the National Weather Service issued a Red Flag warning—a total fire ban—for north central Colorado. The air mass over the Rockies was exceptionally dry, with relative humidity between 5 and 8 percent. Winds exceeded fifteen miles per hour, with gusts of up to thirty miles per hour.

Terry Barton, a thirty-eight-year-old mother of two teenage girls, arrived at eight that morning at the Lake George station, thirty-seven miles northwest of Colorado Springs. Barton had been with the Fire Service for two decades as a part-time seasonal employee, and had recently been awarded provisional full-time status with duties that included patrol and issuing violations and warning notices; her ambition was to eventually work as a fire investigator. That day, she remained at the station with coworkers until 2:00 p.m., then went out on patrol alone. At 4:55 p.m. she called in a fire; she'd smelled smoke from about a mile away and discovered an escaped campfire. On the radio with dispatch she described flame links of 1–2 feet and a grass fire past the trees. She requested an engine. Still linked by radio she made efforts to suppress, shoveling dirt against the base of a Ponderosa pine. But she could not contain the fire—it was now torching in the trees. The Fire Service ordered four fire engines, two airtankers, a five-person hand crew, and two helicopters. By the time the first engine arrived, at around 5:15 p.m., the fire covered over three acres.

A torching fire is one that ignites the crown of trees or shrubs before returning to the surface. A crowning fire is classed as either "dependent" or "running," based on how much its rate of progression varies from what's happening on the ground. A running crown, driven by gusts of wind, is wildly dangerous; flames fly through the treetops. By June 10, when the Forestry Service opened an official investigation, the Hayman Fire had become a running crown. It now covered more than 60,000 acres.

IN THE SMALL meadow where the fire had started, Forest Service Special Agent Kim Jones inspected the burned-out campfire ring, finding three matches in close proximity and gaps in the stones that formed the ring. A large triangle-shaped rock appeared to have been angled away, balanced against a second, smaller rock as if propped; the triangle-shaped rock's outline could be seen in the dirt below. Burn patterns in the grass indicated that the fire had first escaped the ring here. These and other details suggested it might have been set on purpose by Terry Barton. Why would she do such a thing?

On June 10, Jones interviewed Barton onsite. Again she said that she'd smelled smoke and found fire. A second investigator, Paul Steensland, examined the burnt material in the campfire ring. Aside from the matches, it all appeared to be organic.

Investigators reinterviewed Barton twice, each time onsite with videotaped reenactments. Again Barton said she'd smelled smoke, she'd found fire, she'd been the one to call it in. She added that she may have seen a vehicle in the area—perhaps the driver had started the fire?

During the second reinterview, confronted with inconsistencies between her statement and the physical evidence, Barton confessed she'd accidentally started the fire by lighting a two-page letter from her husband in the campfire ring with a single match. Her amended statement read:

> On Saturday June 8, 2002, I left my home and my husband handed me a letter. I wasn't speaking with him and we're going through a divorce. He told me he had burned the divorce papers. He was suppose[d] to sign . . . I left for work at 0800 and took the letter with me. [While on patrol] I guess I started thinking about John. I looked at the letter, but didn't read it. I drove down a dead end spur and then came up the road and saw the campfire ring. I decided that I wanted to get rid of the letter . . . I wasn't thinking about the fire ban. I didn't want to start a fire. I thought the campfire ring was a good place to burn [it].

Barton was in the midst of a messy divorce. Her estranged husband, John, an alcoholic prone to bullying and violent confrontations, had returned home a few days before the fire. The night of June 7, he'd punched a hole in the bathroom door during a heated argument and Barton, fed up, spent the night at a friend's. The following morning she went directly to work.

This scenario cast doubt on Terry Barton's statement. Additionally, John claimed he'd slept on the porch and didn't see her the morning of June 8. He denied giving his wife a letter or burning their divorce papers.

Terry Barton's supervisor told investigators that, on June 15, the day Barton provided her amended statement, she'd confided that John had written that Satan had taken over Barton's life, that she needed to come back to him or the family would all go to hell. She told another worker that John had referred to *her* as Satan. Had she read the letter, after all, or did she think embellishments might further explain her disastrous decision to burn it? A third possibility: Did the letter not even exist?

After watching the paper burn to ash, Barton wrote, she'd left the scene, returning within a few minutes to the clearing. Had she worried the fire wasn't really out, or did she know it couldn't be? In her statement she described approaching the meadow and seeing fire emanating from the campfire ring, sweeping north toward some trees. Investigators estimated the escaped flames reached those trees within thirty seconds.

Barton explained why she'd lied:

I never meant for this to happen, this was an emotional act. When I turned around and seen the fire, I knew it was my fault and I wanted to put it out. I became even more fearful as the fire grew and it became harder to come forward. I was fearful about how I could support my daughters, without a job as a single mother, and if I went to jail my daughters would have to live with my ex-husband who isn't a good person.

Additional testing on the campfire debris showed no recognizable part of a letter or letter-like material. And still investigators could not conclude that the fire had been set on purpose. Samples hadn't been collected for an entire week, and evidence that supported Barton's story might have blown away. Mysteriously, matches from the book Barton gave investigators differed from those found in the campfire ring.

By the time the Hayman Fire was contained, it had resulted in so much destruction that several insurance companies would jointly file a multimillion-dollar suit against the Fire Service, claiming that Barton was negligent in her duties.

In the end, whether the fire was accidental or deliberate didn't matter. On December 6, 2002, Barton signed a deal with prosecutors, pleading guilty to making a false statement, and to "Setting a Fire on Lands of the United States." She was sentenced to twelve years in federal prison and ordered to pay $42.2 million in federal and state restitution. The case was resolved, yet there was a frustrating lack of resolution. Barton never gave an interview, and the discrepancies in her story remained. She served six years before being released in 2008. That same year, during the civil suit brought by insurance companies against the Forest Service, she testified that she'd reconciled with her ex-husband, John.

What might have prompted this unsettling reversal? During the investigation, one of Terry's friends had suggested that the Bartons' teenage daughters might have placed their father's letter in Terry's day pack, seeing it as a love note and a plea for forgiveness. It was never clear whether this actually happened, but it seems possible that Barton, in later reconciling with John, considered her daughters' longing for their lost family. Or maybe it was simply a matter of love. Maybe Barton had decided that she was the one who couldn't live with the void.

IN 2002 ANOTHER recession hit Colorado, and seemingly overnight, customers for Vinnie's furniture restoration dried up. It sent us into a financial panic. I'd applied for an associate professorship in creative writing at Colorado University at Boulder—in those days, with publications, you could teach without an advanced degree—and made it to the final round. I got my hopes up. When they picked another writer, I took it hard. I'd sold a second novel, though, and now anxiously awaited its release in the fall. That book, as happens sometimes, fell off the face of the earth. Whether it deserved this fate, I couldn't say, but the *ifs* were punishing: if no one hears about your novel, no one will read it; if no one reads, no one will buy it; if no one buys, I'll never get the chance to do it again. This depressing chain of reasoning served as a reminder that I needed work. Since losing out on the teaching position, I'd refused to continue as an adjunct, cutting off my nose to spite my face. I'd long since traded graphic design for writing, and the design world, always competitive and now computerized, had passed me by.

That December I took a temporary position with the Public Works Department of the City of Lafayette, a small town east of Boulder. The job entailed administrative support for a three-month, five-mile-long water pipeline project, a joint effort funded by taxpayers after seventeen months of record temperatures and drought. A portion of Boulder Creek, with its valuable spring run-off from the Rockies, would be channeled out to Lafayette's main reservoir.

The city set up my boss and me in a trailer—formerly a sales office for a cemetery—on land abutting the pipeline's route. As if delivered to the site, dead moths an inch thick covered the indoor-outdoor carpeting. Winter air blew through gaps in the walls. Facilities were limited to a single Porta Potty in the yard.

I typed, filed, and manned the phones. I vacuumed; workers tracked in ungodly amounts of mud and debris. I took minutes at chaotic weekly construction meetings where an oddly poetic lingo flew: *eccentric reducer, riprap, grit chamber, corp stop, couplers, swale, spring line.* "Radar mapping indicates a nasty BFR," one of the supervisors said. When I asked what technical situation this referred to, my boss deadpanned, "Big fucking rock."

The job concluded, and I went back to worrying about money. But a seed had been planted: I wanted to write another novel. I had not even a germ of an idea, but there was something about the pipeline—the adventure of excavation, the thrill of water running underground—that told me a story waited. All I had to do was find it.

This realization coincided with our decision to sell the house in Boulder. Increasingly it felt like a place for the rich, a kind of Disneyland. Vinnie's business was still hurting, and who knew when it might recover. We had equity. We could move somewhere more affordable. Somewhere near water. This time, starting over would not be so hard. Amy was enthusiastic about a change, as well, and we hoped she'd consider enrolling for a final year of high school.

Erin had graduated from college and accepted a job for the next year at the American Embassy in Nicaragua. So Vinnie and Amy and I discussed where we might go. I was drawn to the Pacific Northwest, a place gauzy with rain, as saturated as Colorado was dry. Years ago I'd seen *The Goonies*, which was set in Astoria, a small town at the mouth of the Columbia River. Images from the film had stuck in my mind: a boy standing on the porch of an old Victorian that overlooked the river; a wild bicycle ride through the world's greenest trees; a shipwreck stuck for decades on the sands.

In charge of reconnaissance, I flew to Portland, rented a car, and drove two hours west to Astoria. I cruised through in ten minutes flat. The town had 10,000 citizens, two strip joints, several churches and bars, diners and a movie theater, a VFW, and a Safeway. Along the main drag, tourist shops alternated with boarded-up storefronts. Decrepit hundred-year-old houses with prices from the 1970s climbed the emerald hills. I devoured a spaghetti dinner at an

Italian restaurant and, feeling euphoric, took a drunken stroll along the river. Over on the Washington side, the coastal range was covered in snow. The air sparkled but felt liquified. Jagged piles from piers that had once supported a dozen canneries jutted up from the water. A fact I'd picked up over dinner: The mouth of the Columbia was called the Graveyard of the Pacific, with more shipwrecks here than anywhere else on the West Coast. The river's surface might look placid, but the water was cold and the currents lethal.

As the sun dropped, an electrical storm in the brain descended. I saw my new novel whole. In the motel I took page after page of fevered notes. I would fictionalize what had happened to me. I'd write about a woman in the midst of a love affair who underestimates her husband's capacity for revenge. There'd be two young children, a boy and a girl. The husband would stalk his estranged wife, and kidnap the son. There'd be a bar pilot plying the Columbia, Astoria's underground tunnels, watery light on bedroom ceilings. The woman, I decided, would murder her husband while her children slept, stabbing him with a kitchen knife while she was sleepwalking, the plot turning on whether she was faking the condition to get rid of a man she feared above everything.

I RETURNED TO Boulder, and a few months later, our house sold. The deal was perversely contingent on our fixing things the buyers intended to tear out during a remodel before they moved in, so Vinnie stayed in Colorado to work on the punch list and wind down his business. Amy stayed, too; she was enjoying her summer job as a bagger at Ideal Market.

I drove back to Astoria alone, having been given the mission to find us a house. I rented an unfurnished studio in a fourplex overlooking Youngs Bay. I bought a cheap mattress and bedding at Fred Meyer, along with a table and a folding chair. In between real-estate appointments I worked on my novel. From the studio's picture window, I had a view of both the water and the neighborhood's cryptic comings and goings. Across the street, cars idled at all hours in front of an apartment building. A driver, or sometimes a passenger, would get out, climb outside stairs to the second story, and amble along the walkway to an open window. They'd hang an arm down inside then quickly withdraw it, pocketing the purchase before ambling away.

I was in one of my fourplex's two ground-floor units, with a couple of men in their twenties across the hall whom cops rousted on the regular. I sat in my window, typing, looking out at one or another dejected dude being handcuffed on the tiny front lawn. *But Officer.* Above me lived an unseen couple who stayed up all night, bowling, it sounded like, on the linoleum. It made it hard to sleep. A family of six rented the other upstairs unit. The mom, on her knees in the yard, tended obsessively to a flower bed; she seemed exhausted by her feral children, four fair-haired boys so thin and pale the blue veins on their shirtless chests were visible. The oldest was maybe eleven, the youngest five. It was like seeing the same child at different ages. The dad, who appeared to be minimally employed, spent most of his time sitting on the building's front steps, smoking—unlike Boulder, lots of people here smoked—and screaming at his wife and young sons.

I made friends with the littlest boy. With his sticky face and ready smile, he reminded me of Amy when she was that age. Whenever I answered his knock, he'd open with "I'm hungry. Got any bread?" I'd fix him a sandwich and he'd stuff it down while sitting at the table, chattering. One day he told me a story about someone named George, who I took to be the studio's previous tenant. A bird had flown into the room and got itself trapped inside an open dresser drawer. The boy jumped up and hopped around to demonstrate. George, the boy said, had slammed the drawer shut, and the bird's head came clean off. *Bam!* The boy took a bite of his PB&J and said around the gluey mouthful, "It was cool."

FOR A WHILE the writing poured out of me. I slept little but had plenty of energy, and regularly went on miles-long rambles that led to more writing. One day, in the grip of another manic brainstorm, I changed my character's name to Terry—for Terry Barton. I didn't know what to make of Barton, but I was struck by parallels: we both had two daughters; we'd both gone through difficult divorces; we'd both married men who would not let go. We'd both made decisions that changed everything. The name change felt inspired: Terry/Kerry. *Jesus.*

By mid-summer I'd found us a pretty house we could afford, one with a wraparound porch and a view of the Columbia. I handled the paperwork on the sale, and after it closed I moved in. It was quieter in the house, more private, but lonelier. Sleep still eluded me. Storms blew in. The rain drummed ominously. A foghorn boomed through the night, inducing dread. Sometimes a solid whiteness wrapped around everything. It made it impossible to look out at the world. The house had stood for nearly a century, but because of foundation problems the floors slanted, and while we'd known that when we made the offer, living with the slant threw off my inner ear. Getting up in the night I ran into walls, a funhouse effect that might have been a product of my disintegrating psyche. A warning.

Every morning I swept huge juicy-looking spiders from the wraparound porch. I picked blackberries, my fingers bloody from thorns. Walking in town, I saw evil omens. I cowered at a stop sign riddled with bullet holes and averted my gaze from a Confederate flag in a window, concealing who-knew-what inside. Unidentifiable sounds blared from unknown directions. Faces distorted. Astoria was objectively a beautiful place with many kind people, but in my distress it seemed populated by monsters. Afraid, I stopped going out. For a few weeks I obsessively cleaned the house's emptiness, and then, abruptly, the last of my self-sufficiency drained away. I couldn't feel my edges. Food tasted strange, dusty and dry, or rotten, or fishy, or mushy. I stopped eating.

I cried and cried and cried.

I'd never felt suicidal, and didn't now, but for the first time I understood how seductive not existing could be.

Why had I been so determined to pull up stakes?

Why were we leaving people we loved?

What had I done?

I missed my daughters so much I felt sick. Amy, I knew, was all right, she and Vinnie had each other, but Erin was so far away. We did talk on the phone, but rarely, and from her letters I couldn't quite make out her state of mind. As it turned out, she wasn't okay. She suffered at the embassy, felt isolated and fragile and dangerously on edge. Shadows again fell over her. But before I grasped that she was in trouble, the shadows lifted and she was again fine. Was this all just the rhythm of life? Or was it the void?

On the phone with Amy, I listened to her grocery-store adventures. With Vinnie I dissembled. I steadied my voice to ask, "Should I come home?" For the first time ever, he couldn't read me.

"No," he said. "It's a hundred degrees." The repairs on the house were driving him crazy.

"Don't you want help?" I asked. "And what about Amy?"

"We're fine, Kerry. Stay and work on your book."

I can see now that my breakdown was precipitated by financial pressures, by guilt, by a lack of sleep and a loss of appetite, by isolation, and a creative mania that resurrected the worst time in my life. It was also, certainly, a shift in the chemicals in my brain. Any one of these things might have yielded to sensible intervention, but combined they made for a perfect storm.

I should have told Vinnie. I should have flown home. Had I learned nothing? Only: I'd gone from my parents' house to Gil, and from Gil to Vinnie. I'd had children so young. I'd never been alone with my thoughts for more than a day. I wanted to see them, to capture them, to understand. But wanting wasn't enough. They skittered away.

In desperation I took myself to a clinic in town. I sat in a crowded waiting room leaking oily tears. The doctor prescribed two different medications. Within a day they dried me up but left me a zombie.

In the house, I sat in a window, scribbling.

The children sleep, their small faces shining in moonlight.

My novel's protagonist was a murderer.

Her bloody footprints cover the floor.

One day, I read through the pages, shocked to discover that what had seemed so riveting rang luridly false. I'd penetrated neither the situation nor the characters: the husband, who was Gil, and the wife. Who was me.

Or was the husband John Barton, and the wife, Terry?

I looked out at the river and thought about fire, the phrase "torching crowns" evoking both destruction and a race of mythical women, giants of the forest fleeing the scene of a crime with their hair aflame.

Barton's plan to save the forest had failed. My plan to save my family did not. She was a convicted criminal. I might have been, if we'd been caught. Did she, in her secret heart, think of herself as a hero? I'd thought of myself that way in mine. In the next breath, though, I was certain that couldn't be right.

ON THE PHONE Vinnie said, "We're coming, Kerry."

One more week.

"We're coming."

Four days. Three days. Two days. One.

Through the front window, I saw the moving van.

Vinnie and Amy climbed out. They raced up the porch while I opened the door. Then they crushed me. Their arms were warm, their breath was warm. Vinnie's lips breathed life into me. Amy buried her head in the crook of my neck, whispering, *Oh, Mom*.

I saved my little girl once—*didn't I?* And look at her, right here and right now, saving me.

Defiant Heart

We lived in Astoria for a year and a half before two events conspired to send us on another journey. The first was Vinnie's desire to take a voice-acting class. The best city to do this was, naturally, Los Angeles. We rented a place off Craigslist for three months, sight unseen. Amy enlisted in the Navy—that was the second event. We were proud of her, and anxious about her safety. But she was eighteen. The thread that connected her to me was unspooling. What made a mother? Maybe knowing when to let go.

By the time our three months in LA were up, we realized we were happier there. Everything had changed in the years we'd been gone, but it was also exactly the same, a place that ran on creativity and corruption, diversity, division, and sunshine. It felt like home. We rented another apartment and found tenants for the Astoria house. Vinnie snagged a few voiceover gigs. The cost of living was so high he also took a job doing logistics for an interior design firm. I edited freelance and taught night classes at UCLA Extension Writers' Program.

For my novel workshops, I liked a three-part exercise:

Begin with a drawing of where you grew up: a landscape, a house, an apartment. Label each space or room within it and think about what happened in those locations. Here is where your parents had an epic fight about your dad losing his job. Here is where you pitched a baseball through a window. Here is the tree beneath which you lost your virginity. Here is the fire hydrant outside your building that cooled every kid on the block. Now pick one incident to write about for fifteen minutes, something with juice: Go!

Invariably, the work that came out of this exercise was vivid, rich in detail, and emotionally resonant.

The handout included a sketch I'd made of my childhood home, on Micheltorena Street in Silver Lake. It didn't contain all that happened there—it couldn't—yet looking at this drawing never failed to send me back in time.

Since we'd returned to LA, I'd avoided the old neighborhood. Too many memories; I was afraid of what I would feel. But one day, at loose ends, I found myself in that part of town. I gunned it up the familiar hill.

I made a U-turn at the top and parked across the street from my parents' house, in front of the Canfield-Moreno estate, where Gil and I had our wedding reception. I made sure to curb the wheels; at seventeen, I'd lost my first car, a used VW Squareback I'd owned for less than a week, because the parking brake failed—the car had rolled down the hill and smashed into another parked vehicle. Children were playing down there. I was lucky no one was killed.

Two doors up, a neighbor's house still looked like a Beatrix Potter illustration, with a thatched roof and multipaned windows and roses in the front yard. When I was a kid, a young family had lived there. The dad was a handsome attorney, the mom an artist, a freckled redhead with happy crinkles at the corners of her eyes; and they'd had two kids, the older a five-year-old girl, the younger a baby boy who was two. This family moved in different social circles than ours, and the kids were too young to be playmates for me, but my mother used to get up the occasional bridge game with the wife, along with a few other ladies around the way, including a woman named Meryl, who was my friend Jennifer's mom.

The summer of 1968, the neighbor family went off to their annual vacation at Big Bear Lake, and the little boy drowned. The parents, each heading back to their cabin for lunch, took different paths along the water's edge. Each thought their son was with the other.

I remembered how sorry everyone was about the little boy's death, but also how, as the shock wore off, a communal judgement crept in that the wrong child had died. No adult ever came out and said so, at least not to me, but the feeling was palpable. The boy had been bubbly and sweet, full of personality, while his older sister was skittish and dorky and therefore less appealing. Mom and I went to the funeral, and as mourners filed past, I watched the girl be too lightly hugged and too quickly let go. She stood between her parents, making a sound low in her throat, a kind of growling. The dad placed a warning hand on her head. The mom glanced down into her daughter's face and frowned.

A woman came out of my parents' house, which was now, probably, hers. She stood at the top of the stairs, then walked down and made a beeline for my car; she must have seen me sitting there. I straightened up, trying to look like I wasn't casing the joint, only admiring the view.

The woman leaned down and peered through my open window. "Can I help you?"

I hesitated before saying, "I grew up in that house."

"Really?" Her face lit up. "It's changed a lot, huh?"

When our family lived there, it had been a modest two-bedrooms-one-bath, plus a den. White wooden clapboard with black shutters. Since then someone had built a second story, stuccoed the exterior, and put up a wall. The vernacular was modern, the roofline altered.

The house had changed its identity.

"You want to come in?" the young woman asked.

To my surprise, I did.

She gave me a tour. The inside had also been remodeled, but there was still much I recognized. Like the corner of the living room where, when ditching school in eighth grade, I'd hide behind the piano until Mom went to work. Here was the fireplace mantel

I climbed to tease the dog. Here was a dining room table sitting in the same spot ours had, where I'd once drawn my maps; the pine tree on the other side of sliding-glass doors still grew through a hole in the deck. Here was the hallway where Daddy practiced chipping golf balls. When I was little, he used to tell me he had no belly button. He'd let me style his thinning hair with barrettes while he read the newspaper. He gave me spelling words disguised as riddles. I'd forgotten all that. If he'd lived longer, I might have eventually come to appreciate him. . . . Oh, but look, the old Red Room was still a den. My alcove bedroom, on the other hand, was now a landing for a staircase to the second floor. The skinny closet that had once housed Satan was gone, and with it, the shelf where I'd kept the strongbox that held the Polaroid of my son.

TOWARD THE END of that summer when the neighbors' child drowned, my friend Jennifer invited me to spend a three-day weekend at Disneyland to celebrate her eleventh birthday. Her parents would treat. Mom let me go only after extracting a promise from Meryl to take me to a Catholic church in Anaheim on Sunday. This must have flummoxed Meryl. It was Jennifer's birthday; also, the family were atheists.

Sometimes I didn't know what to make of them. For one thing, Jennifer's parents were affectionate in ways mine definitely were not, often disappearing in the middle of the day to "nap." There was no alcohol in their house. No one smoked. No one argued. The kitchen smelled of cookies baking, and there were family art projects and musical evenings. I was aware that Meryl got on Mom's nerves. She'd told me once that the woman reminded her of a childhood friend from New York, a girl with artful makeup and sculpted curls and an air of perfection so infuriating that Mom one day packed a giant snowball into her fist and mashed it in her friend's face.

I'd waited at our front door, looking out for Jennifer's car. I didn't want anyone to come up and ring the bell. Mom, hungover and still in her robe, stood beside me. Daddy was holed up in the bedroom, dead drunk.

Meryl pulled into the driveway and tapped the horn. Jennifer peered up through the windshield. Mom drew a hand through my hair, but I ducked and took off down the stairs.

I thought everyone else's family was better than ours. Other people loved each other more. They had more fun. The parents *indulged*. At our house there was no indulgence and precious little fun.

Not everything at Jennifer's was perfect, of course. Her older sister, a model Scout, gymnast, and piano prodigy, used to force us into a closet and make us strip naked so she could scrape our buttocks bloody with the serrated edge of a tape dispenser. Maybe, I thought, that's what came of being an atheist. I'd been ecstatic to learn she would not be coming to Disneyland.

Once inside the park, Meryl and Davis planted themselves on a bench in the shade. They gave Jennifer and me money and a book of tickets, and set us loose. It was a gift of independence. We rode the Matterhorn bobsled as often as we could stand to wait in line. Same with Pirates of the Caribbean, and the Submarine Voyage, Autopia, the Jungle Cruise, the Pack Mules, It's a Small World, and Mr. Toad's Wild Ride. We climbed the Swiss Family Robinson's Treehouse and took the Mark Twain Riverboat over to Tom Sawyer Island. Hot and tired, we holed up in the theater on Main Street to watch *Great Moments* with an Audio-Animatronic Mr. Lincoln.

For three days, we stayed until closing. We ate out every meal, hamburgers and french fries, and for dessert, popsicles. Even having to attend Mass on Sunday wasn't that bad, because afterward Jennifer's parents took us out for chocolate-chip pancakes topped with whipped cream. We went to a bookstore, too—the adults needed more reading material for their bench in the shade—and Meryl let me pick out a book.

I snatched up a young adult novel called *The Defiant Heart*, drawn to it by the cover illustration of a long-haired, violet-eyed teenage beauty in a scarlet shirtdress. I carried the book through the park and read it in the car on the drive home. The heroine was an orphan sent to live with her very strict aunt who had firm ideas about her niece's behavior. The story felt romantic. How alone the girl was, how deeply misunderstood. And, as expected, there was a boy.

When Jennifer's parents dropped me off late Sunday night, I ran up the stairs, my overnight bag banging against my hip. I was so sunburnt my cheekbones ached. In my arms I cradled *The Defiant Heart* and a watercolor portrait by a genuine Disneyland artist, another gift from Meryl. I was charmed by the way the artist had painted me, with smooth rather than frizzy pigtails, an inaccurately upturned nose, and a clear light in my hazel eyes.

Our front door was unlocked, the house dark. I called out but no one answered. The dog was upon me, excited beyond the joy of reunion, feinting and returning. I followed him into the gloomy living room, where I found Mom curled in her blue armchair, smoking a cigarette.

Dying to show her my loot, I moved to turn on a lamp.

"Leave it," she said.

When I went to kiss her, she sat motionless. I still didn't see that something was wrong. I babbled on about Disneyland, about all the fun I'd had, the food and the rides and the portrait and the book, which I *loved*.

"Where did you get those shorts?" Mom interrupted.

I looked down. The shorts I had on were Jennifer's. She was smaller and slighter than me, and they were tight.

"I spilled soda," I explained.

"What do you think you're up to?"

"I—" I stopped, bewildered. "I'm not up to anything."

"Don't you argue with me."

Mom's voice thrummed. She was very angry. She often was. Sometimes I knew why, sometimes I did not, but on this night there was a hostility I'd never before heard, the source of which I could not identify.

"Sexy," she said. "That's what you think you are."

"What? No. What do you mean?"

"You know," she said.

Disgust. That's what I heard in Mom's voice. I disgusted her. The shock of it hit me in the chest. I was a crier, a kid who wept dramatically over everything—Mom often called me Sarah Bernhardt, her accusations of fakery only increasing the flood—but that night I didn't cry. I could hardly breathe.

"Mary Alice!" Mom hissed.

Mary Alice was her old childhood friend, she of the artful makeup and sculpted curls, the only child of a couple who worked in vaudeville. The family had lived in the same building as Mom's, on New York's Upper West Side, and the two girls often visited back and forth, sleeping over and staying up late, whispering in a shared bed. Mom had told me Mary Alice was the smartest person she'd ever known, the most talented, the funniest, but at some point during their adolescence they'd fallen out, and she'd stopped loving her friend. When I asked why, all Mom would say was that something had happened to Mary Alice. She'd had to *go away*. Mary Alice was *bad*.

At eleven, I didn't know what that meant. Within five years I would. Within five years it would be said of me that something had happened, that I'd had to go away, that I was bad.

I watch my eleven-year-old self tripping toward Mom in the dark, radiating happiness. How she must have panicked at those tight shorts. All that nascent sexuality. Trouble now, trouble later, trouble forever, maybe. I was only a child, her child, but also the child of a woman known only because she'd given birth to me. Which was stronger, nature or nurture? An unanswerable question. But maybe, in giving voice to her fears, Mom planted a seed. Maybe, because she'd named me, I became what was named.

"Go to bed," she told me. The words coming out of her mouth dry as dirt.

It wasn't bedtime, but I didn't argue. I didn't even want to. Mom often accused me of being an itch, of overstaying my welcome, of asking too many questions and demanding explanations; but that night, I could not wait to get away.

THE OWNER OF the house took me out onto the deck, sat me down in a redwood chaise, and served me a glass of wine. The woman worked in show biz and all through her twenties she'd saved. She'd bought during the economic downturn in the early 1990s. "The mortgage was cheaper than my rent," she said, settling in. It may have been the last time that was possible.

My parents had owned chaises like these. I remembered how Mom would wake me up late at night and bring me outside to sit beside her. It would be winter, the air cool and dry; it would be summer, the air soft with smog. The darkness felt sentient. Smell of eucalyptus trees. Close your eyes, Kerry, she'd say, and tell me what you hear. Wind in the branches. Traffic on the Hollywood Freeway. Crying cats. A hoot owl. Voices, very faint, coming from the other side of the reservoir. Listen harder, she'd say. But I never entirely grasped what she wanted, so I'd open my eyes to the sky.

"I love it, but it drops tons of needles," the owner said. She meant the pine tree that grew up through the deck and towered over the house. "Clogs up the gutters."

"Yes," I agreed. "Yes."

"Thank you," I added nonsensically, as another memory rushed in.

THE MORNING AFTER I returned from Disneyland, Mom decided we'd sweep the roof after breakfast. The choked gutters were causing leaks, tea-colored stains in the ceiling that looked like maps of undiscovered countries.

Mom got our splintered old ladder from the basement while I went to the garage for brooms. I watched her drag the ladder into a narrow space between our house and the neighbors'; because of the hill, the distance up to the roof was shortest there. Even so, she had to balance the ladder atop a retaining wall.

Mom steadied the ladder's sides. She looked at my bare feet. "You have no goddamn sense. Go put sneakers on."

When I returned properly shod, I climbed. At the top I crawled onto the roof, sat down hard, and scooted around on my butt, working myself to the edge. I leaned over. Blood pounded in my cheeks as Mom fed me first one broom, then the other. Then she climbed up. No one held the ladder for her.

She set me to sweeping over the dining room, while she took the eaves above the kitchen. The day was windy, the treetops shivering. We pushed pine needles to the edge and swept them over, and falling they looked like pitched hay. I felt the height as a sea-sicky squirm in my stomach but soon got used to it.

Mom worked the back of the house. I moved to the part of the roof that covered my parents' bedroom. For the first time in three days, I thought about Daddy behind his closed door. And for the first time ever, I concluded that this was Mom's fault.

When I was younger, we'd been so close I felt her moods in my body, a wiggly optimism when she was in good spirits, a drowned weight when she was suffering. Over the last year, though, a rift had opened. I moved the broom briskly over the shingles. Maybe Mom drove Daddy to drink with her terrible temper, her fault-finding, her unbending preference for God over any man. I'd once seen her break a glass on Daddy's head, so much blood pouring from his scalp I thought she'd killed him. He was so drunk, the injury didn't even register. Poor Daddy. She was always screaming at him. No wonder he couldn't, or wouldn't, see me.

The roof was steepest over the living room, the drop down to the ground on that side more than twenty feet. There were fewer pine needles here, but I swept assiduously all the same. When I was done I straddled the precarious peak. My chest opened, my head swam, my blood fizzed. I felt weirdly buoyant, and if wishing made flying possible, I would've been off. Looking out was like seeing into the future, the view wide, San Gabriel to Catalina Island. The wind—the famed Santa Ana—had moved the brown cloud out to sea. Below me, the reservoir shined blue as a mountain lake.

My hair whipped around my face. I was standing too close to

the edge. I looked over my shoulder. Mom was watching me. It made me angry, the way she leaned on her broom handle, a hand shielding her eyes. She was angry, too, angry at me.

Vibrating. Pulsing. Shimmering.

THE NEIGHBORS WHO lost their son never had another biological child, but six years later they adopted a two-year-old out of foster care, a boy who had been abused. The parents came alive in a way they had not been in ages, palpably full of hope.

In recent decades, the joy of those who adopt has been reassessed in light of adoptees' unacknowledged grief and lifelong struggles with identity. But even now, we are expected to be grateful above all. Adoptees are at risk for mental health disorders, separation anxiety, depression, and ADHD. They may feel guilt and shame. They may disproportionately fear rejection. The sense of loss lingers, and succeeding losses can be felt more keenly.

In 1974, all we knew about the neighbor's adopted son was that he'd been damaged and needed rescue. The parents had done a good deed while expanding their family.

And while I was a senior at a new high school with nowhere to be on Saturday nights, I babysat this boy and his sister. I'd only recently surrendered my son, and was weeks away from encountering Gil, who would be my future.

By coincidence the neighbors' new baby had the same name I'd given my child: Joseph—Joey.

I coddled this little boy, played with him endlessly, bathed him, and fed him treats. When he put his arms around my neck, I wanted to cry. I mostly ignored his older sister, who'd turned into a moody preteen prone to unnerving laughter and public masturbation. She wanted me to play Parcheesi with her, but I made excuses.

I fixed her dinner and set her up at the dining-room table, but she ate alone. She asked me to read to her, but I wouldn't do it. Instead we watched TV. I pretended there was room for only two on the couch. Me and the baby. The older girl sat on the floor and glared at the screen and snuck a hand into her panties.

And I thought that maybe it was true that the wrong child had drowned. Well, my heart had been flattened, and I was young myself and so lonely, and I felt, I suppose, that the world owed me. Blinded by the little boy in my arms, I could not see that I was doing another child damage, unaware that there was in me an as-yet-unrecognized potential for cruelty.

17

The Ninth Man

I had tried to stop obsessing about the past, but how do you let go of a story you've been telling yourself for years, when there is no ending? I still thought about Gil, and every now and then, I googled him. The only thing that ever came up was his failed appeal to the New York State Supreme Court regarding his conviction on gun possession. Was this lack of information reassuring? I didn't know.

In 2006 an attorney friend in Colorado, who thought that knowing where Gil lived might put my mind at ease, referred me to a private investigator. The PI tracked him from New York to Santa Maria, California; I'd long assumed he'd stayed on the East Coast, and learning he might be less than two hundred miles away was alarming. The PI, however, had found no listed phone number, no street address, and no utilities in Gil's name—it was so classically Gil. He'd popped up solely via a "known associate," a term that smacked of law enforcement. The information was out of date by more than a year. How likely was it that, if Gil had ever lived with this man, he still did? I typed in the associate's name, but there were no hits. I typed in the address and called up a Google Maps street view of a nondescript buff-colored condo, 1970s-vintage, with a narrow entry and an oddly angled roofline. I tried to picture Gil inside it. He'd turned sixty-eight in January, so I gave him thinning gray hair. Recalling his bad back from testimony at the New York trial, I planted him in an easy chair, watching TV, a cane close to hand.

What would he watch? Not sports—he hated sports. The news, maybe. The news, definitely. I zoomed in on the street and moved the camera view along. The asphalt looked hot. There wasn't much greenery.

And I thought: I could drive up to Santa Maria. Park a half block away and watch the condo's front door. Or I could ask Vinnie to do it. I could hire someone. The PI had suggested contacting a local detective agency to finish the job. But I was afraid of stirring the pot, afraid the mere act of looking would alert Gil and allow him, somehow, to find me.

So, once again, I told myself, *Let it go.*

IN 2008 ERIN and Amy came to visit us in LA for the Christmas holidays. Erin, now twenty-eight, had graduated from law school in Washington, DC, and passed the bar, and was working at a good firm. Amy, at twenty-four, had entered her sixth year of service in the Navy; she was soon heading overseas. Who knew when we'd all be together again.

We opened gifts on Christmas Eve. The girls presented Vinnie with a wrapped package that looked from its size and shape like a paperback book. It turned out to be a guide to adoption in California; after twenty years as their stepfather, they wanted Vinnie to become their legal dad. Erin, as the family attorney, said she'd handle the paperwork and set proceedings in motion. Vinnie cried, of course, which made me cry. All four of us were bawling. Overall, it was an emotional holiday.

After dinner—in honor of Mom I cooked prime rib, mashed potatoes and creamed spinach, biscuits, and pumpkin pie—the girls suggested a walk. I begged off, pleading exhaustion.

I sank into the couch. The apartment felt peaceful, quiet. I sat in the silence for a while before reaching for the adoption guide on the coffee table. I flipped through. What would be required of us? Would we all be under oath? My mind turned, as it had for twenty years, to our forged identities. Would the court need to see birth certificates, and if so, how closely would they review them? I still kept important documents in my old strongbox, stashed here in a locked secretary: my passport in my old name, old drivers' licenses for both Vinnie and me, our Social Security cards and birth certificates, both the originals and the forgeries I'd concocted years ago. I pulled out the faked birth certificates and inspected them. We'd never get away with it now, I thought.

Now, because of the internet, everyone trailed staggering amounts of data wherever we went, with myriad ways for interested parties to disinter the information. And while we didn't all live online, those of us who did were constantly dropping clues. Your social media accounts broadcast your profession and hobbies, the names of relatives, coworkers, friends, lovers, and pets; they exposed quirks of personality and the state of your health. Your face was there for all to peruse. Given a name, date of birth, and a Social Security number, a good investigator could uncover every job you'd ever had, every address you'd ever lived at, every name you'd ever used. They could sort through your relatives' and friends' names and addresses, too. They could search the photos you'd posted online and retrieve identifying data from your camera, and from other pictures your camera might have taken, and they could follow those threads. If someone wanted you badly enough, all they had to do was sit back and wait. Because, eventually, unable to endure the isolation, you would contact your brother or your cousin or your childhood best friend.

As indeed, eventually, we had done.

An audio cassette sat at the bottom of the strongbox. I fished it out and read its handwritten label: *Gil, June 1989*. This was the recording of the phone conversation I'd had with him when he kidnapped Amy. In all these years I'd never listened to it. I wouldn't now. But I did wonder: What about Gil? The adoption—as the birth father, where did he fit in? I returned to the legal handbook and searched the index. The relevant section reassured me. Because the girls were adults, there was no need for Gil to relinquish his parental rights. *Parental rights.* The phrase made me queasy.

Vinnie and the girls returned from their walk. We sat up a while longer, then went off to bed. But I had trouble sleeping. At around four a.m. on Christmas Day, I gave up. I got up and went out to the living room.

I admired the impressive mess, clothing and shoes strewn over the floor, dessert plates licked clean of pie, presents littering the coffee table. The girls had drawn the blinds, and yellow streetlight crept in around the edges. Conked out on an air mattress, they huddled together, still as stones under blankets, faces burrowed into their pillows. Where were they right now—were they dreaming? I had an urge to shake them, to see if they breathed, and I laughed at myself. The sound startled me, but they slept on. I slipped away.

In the kitchen I made coffee. I fixed a cup and carried it to my office, where I booted the computer and immediately googled Gil's name. After the PI's report, I'd made an effort to stop doing this, so it had been a while. A million-plus hits came up on the screen. I quickly scrolled through. Nothing jumped out. I'd only ever found two items about Gil, both related to his 1993 arrest and conviction in New York. I'd read those documents so many times, I didn't bother to click on them now.

I typed in his old aliases, the names on the driver's licenses he'd used for his scams way back when. Search results here were more interesting—a professor at Rutgers, a councilman in Biloxi, a dog groomer in San Francisco. There was no way to tell if any one of the more ambiguous hits might be him.

I added "Santa Maria" to the search of Gil's name, reducing the results to just two. My pulse kicked up, my mouth went dry—I hadn't expected to find anything. I clicked on the first link and opened an article from the *Santa Maria Times* dated August 26, 2008.

IDENTITY RELEASED ON BODY FOUND IN PARK

The Santa Maria Police Department has released the name of a man found dead in July in Central Plaza Park on North Broadway.

Police were initially investigating the death of Gilbert W_____, an elderly transient, as suspicious based on the position of the body and some of his property being strewn about.

However, they have since said that Gilbert W_____ appears to have died of natural causes.

I ran yet another search, this one from within the publication, adding a string of terms—"body," "Central Park Plaza," "death"— but minus Gil's name. That coughed up an earlier article, dated July 28, 2008:

BODY FOUND IN PARK

Santa Maria Police officers spent Sunday investigating the death of a man found in [sic] about 8:23 a.m. Sunday in Central Plaza Park 100 N. Broadway.

. . . [O]fficers are investigating the death as suspicious.

The identity and age of the victim was not available at press time Sunday.

There was also a photograph.

I counted eight men: three in street clothes, two in tan sheriff's uniforms, three in police blues. There was a swath of green grass, a white T-bone of concrete walkway, a stretch of yellow crime-scene tape. A leafy tree, its roots exposed in a circle of dirt. The tree's branches threw shadows onto a yellow blanket, the blanket covering what could only be a body. When I zoomed in, the photo pixelated, losing detail; the larger it got, the less I could see. Yet even blown up, the body under the blanket looked small, which I knew it was not, and defenseless, which I'd never imagined. Which made it nine, I supposed, men, in the photograph.

I wanted to know how he'd died. Vinnie would want to know, too. And the girls. Gil's daughters. They would always be his—as my son would always be mine—no matter how much they loved Vinnie. Later, when I told them he was gone, their response confounded me: dry-eyed, unsentimental relief.

I was relieved, too. After twenty years of living in fear, how could I not be?

I was unprepared for the grief.

18

According to the Map

New Years came and went. Vinnie returned to work and the girls went back to their lives. Adoption proceedings were scheduled for March. Erin was flying in from DC, but Amy, overseas, would miss the hearing; she'd sign paperwork electronically. I took on a new editing job. But over the next couple of months, the shock of Gil's death gave way to grinding dissatisfaction, so in February I emailed the Santa Barbara County coroner's office, looking for answers about Gil. A detective wrote back and we made arrangements to meet. I drove up to Santa Maria alone, by choice—I needed to do this alone.

The sheriff's station sat at the south end of town. I followed a eucalyptus-lined road that wound into a half-empty parking lot, then waited outside the building's entrance, as I'd been instructed to do. I had a view through glass doors into the sheriff's office entry, which looked deserted. Several minutes passed before I started for the doors. My reflection in the glass stopped me. The coroner's detective was meeting me on the sly and I'd been told to *wait*. So I sat on a low wall that surrounded a tree. I held my bag in my lap. The leaves above me were very green.

Finally, a heavyset man in his forties emerged from the double doors. He wore civilian clothes and had close-cropped dark hair—was this the coroner's detective? The man approached, a question in his eyes. I stood to greet him and stuck out a hand. "Karen Palmer."

"Yes," he said. "How can I help you, Ms. Palmer? What are you looking for?"

In my email, I'd explained that I was Gil W____'s ex-wife, that although we'd divorced a long time ago, I wanted to know what had happened to him.

"I'm not sure where to begin," I said now.

The detective said, "Just go ahead and jump in."

"Okay. Well, the newspaper said police suspected foul play. Do you know why they thought that?"

"I'm afraid I can't give you those details."

I flushed. The detective was under no obligation to tell me anything. "Do you need to see ID?" I asked anxiously.

"Sure. If you want to show me."

I dug around in my bag and got out my wallet, slid out my driver's license, and handed it over. While he inspected it, I pulled out a large envelope and carefully emptied its contents onto the wall. I picked up a photograph of Gil from his army days and passed it over, and a shot of him from the 1970s, when we were first dating, and one with the girls. I passed over a document I'd printed off the internet, Gil's appeal of his 1992 conviction for illegal possession of a weapon. For good measure, I passed over the flyer Vinnie and I made when Gil kidnapped Amy. The detective looked at that one with interest, while I explained, as well as I could given how nervous I was, how when I left him, my former husband lost his mind. I ran through the substance abuse, the death threats, and Amy's kidnapping. I told the detective about the gun. Then I said I'd changed my identity. I did not tell him I'd done this illegally, and I wondered: Would he know?

"I was terrified of him." The words hung there, sounding weak in a way I could not define. Frustrated, I said, "I still am."

The detective sighed. He looked away, thinking. "His belongings were scattered around the body," he said. "Looked like there might've been a struggle. But they decided he'd thrown the stuff around himself." He paused. "While in extremis. The autopsy confirmed he died of natural causes."

"Which means what?"

"Heart attack." The detective scrutinized me, then added, "You had good reason to be scared." He passed the photos back. "Wait here."

He returned to the station with my ID, entering via an unmarked side door. He was gone for what felt like a long time. Was he looking me up in some database, running a record search? Was he checking marriage licenses or Social Security? What might he learn? More time passed. I figured he wasn't coming out. I was a suspicious character, unworthy of information. This detective was the first and only law enforcement official I'd spoken to since we ran. My heart rabbited in my chest, and I wanted badly to leave, but the detective had my driver's license. I was on the verge of darting back to the car anyway, when he came out the side door. I forced myself to sit still. He walked toward me, a heavy-footed gait. He held my ID in one hand.

He passed back my driver's license. I took it too eagerly, slipped it into my wallet, and dropped that into my bag.

Again he sat.

He reached into a jacket pocket, pulled out a business-size envelope, and shook out two small black-and-white copies of photographs. He passed them over. I held them in my palm like eggs plucked from a mama bird's nest. The photos looked vaguely like school portraits. I couldn't quite take them in. It was like staring desperately at a critical notice in a foreign language.

"They're mug shots," the detective said.

"Oh," I said. "*Oh*."

"Your former husband was well known to Santa Maria law enforcement. Over the last four years, he was arrested eighteen times."

"Eighteen! Can you . . . Can you tell me what for?"

"I can't. I can say the charges were all related, one way or another, to chronic substance abuse."

He pointed at one of the pictures. "Look here, they had to prop him up to take this."

The photo came into focus. It was Gil, all right, glaring belligerently into the camera. His hair stuck out in greasy clumps, and several days' worth of salt-and-pepper stubble covered his chin. His face looked gaunt, his neck baggy, his eyes baggy, his cheeks creased. The smiley lips were downturned. Several buttons of a long-sleeved dress shirt were undone, and the collar lay askew. Liver spots dotted Gil's bony chest.

But *his eyes*. Staring into them, I felt a familiar stab of fear. I brought the mug shot closer. What was I looking at here? Fury and threat? Or rank dejection?

"He was—" The detective began again. "He resisted arrest. He assaulted a police officer. They wanted to take him to the hospital because he showed signs of severe alcohol poisoning, but he refused. So he went to jail."

That sounded like Gil.

"As I said, he'd been there before. He didn't like it."

"I'll bet," I said.

I turned my attention to the second photograph, clearly an earlier one. Gil looked better nourished here, heavier in the face and neck. His hair had been buzzed down to a half-inch of growth. It emphasized his jowls. He wore the same button-down, the fabric darker and cleaner, the collar less frayed.

I glanced at the detective. "What else can you tell me?"

"Well, one of his arrests—he got caught up in something up in the hills."

What hills? Santa Maria was flat as a plank. But no, there were hills some miles to the west, dividing the valley from the coast.

"Cops broke up a bunch of teenagers out raising hell. Your ex-husband was there. The kids let him party with them in exchange for buying booze."

Jesus Christ. That, too, sounded like Gil.

"What were they doing?" I asked.

"Nothing good." The detective shrugged. "The last year or so he lived off and on in Central Plaza Park. Had a whole set-up there. A tent. A hibachi."

A *hibachi*?

"He rented a post office box at a mail store in the mall across the street. I'd guess he used it to collect his Social Security checks. Probably used the bathrooms in the mall, too, to clean up . . . sometimes, he worked at a car wash for cash."

I didn't know what to say.

The detective took this as a signal that our conversation was over. He stood. I stood as well.

"Thank you," I blurted. I was crying now. They weren't big tears, only the kind that seep from the corners of your eyes.

"Look," the detective said. "There's nothing you could've done. Whatever happened in the marriage, you weren't the cause of him going downhill. In my experience, alcoholics who refuse to stop drinking head in one direction. You did the right thing to get away."

AFTER LEAVING THE sheriff's station, I drove up Broadway, Santa Maria's main thoroughfare, to the intersection with East Main. I parked the car and walked across the street to Central Plaza Park, where Gil had died. I'd looked it up on Google Maps, in both street and satellite view, but in person it seemed smaller, more like a pocket park. Gil had once enjoyed privacy; here there was none. The traffic on Broadway was heavy. Where would he have pitched a tent? I noted the small gazebo, the water feature, some decorative boulders, a few trees. A concrete path cut through the grass.

I'd printed out the photo from the story in the *Santa Maria Times* and wandered around with it, trying to locate the tree under which his body was found.

After two circuits I approached the park's only other occupant. An old man on a bench had surrounded himself with bulging black garbage bags. He sat hunched, rocking as if cold. I moved closer, cleared my throat, and asked if he remembered a man named Gil who'd lived here in the park last summer.

The old man wouldn't look at me. I tried a few more times, but he did not want to talk.

I gave up and wandered again. I checked perspectives against the newspaper photo, settling finally on a patch that looked right. There was that building in the background, the one with the yellow canopy. And there was the tree trunk with its knobs and branches in the right places, its roots exposed in a circle of dirt.

I stood swaying. But soon I felt foolish. I brought my arms up and hugged myself. That felt foolish, too. I didn't know what to do, so I sat down cross-legged on the grass. Then I laid myself out. The ground was bumpy beneath me. The grass itched my bare arms and the back of my neck. I stared at the sky, a mosaic of blue between branches and leaves, and felt monumentally unsatisfied.

On the drive home, I grew agitated. I came into the apartment like the wind.

Vinnie was in the kitchen, making sauce. A pot bubbled with tomatoes and garlic; a frying pan sizzled with browning sausages.

"What happened?" he asked.

I told him.

"Was it enough, Kerry?"

It was and it wasn't. I didn't know.

"When will it be enough?"

"I don't know. Never, probably."

And Vinnie kissed me.

What can I say about love? How can I ever convey a depth of feeling? All I can show you is the warmth of our kitchen, filled with fragrant steam. All I can give you is the sound of Vinnie breathing. The rise and fall of his chest against mine. The warmth of his arms, the feeling of utter safety. And desire; desire in the moment and desire in memory, desire that rushes or meanders or runs underground, only to surface when least expected with force and full joy.

THE FOLLOWING WEEK I climbed back in the car, headed this time to the Santa Barbara County Courthouse. I wanted to view whatever records they had there on Gil. I received a printout of case numbers, criminal counts and their various resolutions. I asked the clerk for the files, then waited. When she returned, she told me I could make no copies. I could, however, take notes.

The record reflected what the coroner's detective had told me: Gil had been arrested eighteen times. His offenses included misdemeanors for unlawful camping, parole violations, obstruction, property effacement, disorderly conduct, petty theft, and resisting arrest. There were a few felonies: driving while under the influence, assault, and burglary, also a mysteriously dropped charge for possession of a firearm. Altogether, over four years Gil spent more than a year in the Santa Maria jail. His final term ended on July 23, 2008, only five days before he was found dead in the park.

A couple of artifacts in with the files seemed like they'd been left there by mistake: two sets of notes made by clinical psychologists that could not have been meant for public consumption. Each psychologist had evaluated Gil's mental competence to accept a plea deal or stand trial.

The first examination took place in early 2007 in connection with charges for burglary and petty theft. Gil, apparently in bad shape when arrested, had refused to see a doctor and was taken to a holding cell at the jail. I wondered if this incident matched up with the photo the coroner's detective had shown me, where Gil was propped up and glaring. The psychologist described the defendant as an older man dressed in an orange jumpsuit and wearing shackles. The defendant was "malodorous" and "poorly groomed," with messy hair and several days' growth of beard. His affect was "rambling," "disorganized," "circuitous," and "easily derailed." The psychologist noted that Gil was particularly reluctant to sit.

In answer to a series of questions, he said he'd been born in New York City and been married twice and had several children. He said he'd spent his adult career in construction, which wasn't true. He denied ever having received mental health treatment. He denied feelings of depression or suicidal ideation. He denied suffering from hallucinations.

This all upset me, but it was not surprising. I read on.

Gil claimed to have served in Vietnam in the infantry as an "FO," a forward observer. He told a lengthy story about having been a prisoner of war. This was stolen valor, a bold lie; he'd spent his entire tour in Germany during peacetime. Vietnam vets, I knew, were well represented among the homeless. Gil must have gleaned details from someone he met on the street. It was probably a useful tool to garner sympathy and to explain the extent of his fall. Maybe it just made it easier for him to live with himself.

The psychologist noted that though Gil's long-term memory was relatively intact, he repeated himself, often several times in a row. His short-term memory was near nonexistent. He exhibited signs and symptoms of dementia, likely related to alcohol use and abuse. He knew the date but not the day of the week. He did not appear to understand the nature and purpose of the proceedings against him. On the other hand, he was savvy enough to insist that "associates" had led him astray.

That, too, sounded like Gil.

He told the psychologist he'd consumed alcohol all his life and drank every day. He was living exclusively on Social Security. He usually spent early-morning hours running errands. In the afternoon he bought the *LA Times*. That jumped out at me—for years, I'd sat across from him at the kitchen table while he read the paper. When he was done catching up on the news, he said, he drank himself to sleep.

The quotidian details killed me. Gil had gone from being a business owner, a husband and a father, to prison, to being an ex-convict, to homelessness and a lengthening criminal record. But it seemed he remained who he'd always been. His core personality never changed.

A YEAR LATER, in February 2008, a second psychologist had interviewed Gil. This time the related charge was for "petty theft with prior jail term." Again, there was a description: thinning hair, scraggly beard, a blue jumpsuit, no socks. The psychologist noted that Gil's mood during the interview was tense, his affect "restricted."

I skimmed the biography. Born in Manhattan, parents deceased, two marriages, two divorces, kids. Drafted in 1961. Again Gil claimed he'd served in Vietnam; he couldn't recall when he was discharged. "You don't remember things after being tortured," he explained. After getting out of the army, he'd owned a business in Los Angeles, telemarketing office supplies. He'd worked construction, too. He'd had no problems whatsoever with his career, and had been healthy for most of his life. He denied any history of psychiatric problems. He denied receiving treatment or using medication. "I'm not a medicine person." In contrast with the 2007 interview, he denied a history of substance abuse, saying only "I drink socially." He did acknowledge that "ages ago" he'd had a single DUI, while also admitting that his current charges were alcohol related. But he couldn't recall when he'd been arrested or how long he'd been in jail. Recently, he'd stopped cooperating with his court-appointed attorney and was considering representing himself at trial.

Again, none of this surprised me. Gil had always lied about his drinking—it was the honesty in his first interview that was unusual. As for representing himself at trial, well, he always did believe he was the smartest one in the room.

The second psychologist concluded that the defendant's mental status was compromised, his cognitive deficits chronic and consistent with longstanding alcohol abuse; impairment included poor memory function, poor judgment, and impaired insight, with a pattern of extensive talk about subjects tangential to the questions, and requests that questions be repeated. This, the psychologist noted, was a common tactic used to cover compromised memory function. The psychologist felt that treating Gil with antipsychotic medication was unnecessary, as he presented with "sufficient capacity" to accept a plea, while also noting that his mental illness precluded meaningful participation in any defense.

The report ended with the opinion that Gil did not present a significant risk to himself, nor to the health and well-being of those around him.

I had to think about that. Surely Gil had been a risk to himself. He'd apparently come close to dying of alcohol poisoning, and without intervention had been at serious risk of drinking himself to death. Which is exactly what happened. He'd been driving around intoxicated for decades. I had no doubt that what was in the record was only a fraction of what he'd gotten up to. Whether he was at that time still capable of causing harm to others was a trickier question. It was hard to believe he was harmless. He was an injured animal, and an injured animal can kill.

I paged through the reports one last time, reading here and there, looking for things I might have missed. I found a few lines in the 2008 interview, buried in the biographical information I'd earlier skimmed.

Married 1968, 3 kids. She initiated divorce after 6 years. 2nd marriage (about 4 years later). 2 children, can't recall.

I stared at the words—*what* could he not recall? How many children he'd had with me? Or the children themselves?

I think now that the ambiguity I read into this came as much from my state of mind as the words on the page. Or it might've been due to a glitch in the psychologist's notes, maybe an incomplete transcription. What I wanted to know, what I could never know, was whether my taking the girls had destroyed Gil's memories of his daughters. They'd been so young when we ran, and he'd lived a life since so removed from ours it might have taken place on another planet.

He'd told the psychologist that his first wife—that would be Rita—had initiated their divorce, but beyond the fact of our marriage, I wasn't mentioned. For twenty years I'd thought of Gil every day. Was it possible he'd long since forgotten me?

FOR MORE THAN a week my notes from the courthouse files sat in a pile of paperwork on a dining-room chair. Occasionally, I'd dig them out and look through them. The arrest record boiled down to that list of case numbers and counts and the sad facts of sentencing; it felt bloodless. But in the psychologists' reports, I heard Gil's voice, if faintly. I didn't know what I was looking for, only that I hadn't found it.

Eventually, I gave up and stashed the whole mess in the secretary.

Before locking the door, I pulled out my strongbox and opened it up. I dug through, heart racing, and fished out the cassette recorded twenty years ago.

Held in the hand, it weighed almost nothing.

Maybe it was time to listen to it, to hear him again, as if for the first time. This recording might be the only place I'd find Gil. And with him, maybe, myself.

A Reckoning

The sound of his voice. The easy familiarity, the intimacy. The New York accent he never lost that reminded me of Mom and Daddy. Twenty years after this recording was made, it felt like he was in the room with me.

You see how easy it was for me to take her? I could do it again and again and again. Wake up to reality, Kerry. Wake up! There's no way you can prevent it. And I don't care who's looking for me. Do you have the police there now? No, you know better. I'd just get violent. I don't give a fuck. Talking to them doesn't mean garbage. They can't prove it, they can't do anything, and they don't want to be bothered anyway. Until you kill somebody. Then they listen to you. I'm telling you, I've been absolutely insane. Suicidal, maniacal. I hate. I am full of hate. I want to be a prick so bad, just bury you in the ground, and break you to nothing, and break Vinnie to nothing. But I'm a good person, I'm not cruel, I've always been kind to other people, and I always want to be kind. My hand was forced. But I gotta get what I want. Am I gonna get what I want? Why won't you just let me have what I want? I can't go on like this. I either have to kill somebody and get it over with, and then I'll be able to relax, or I get my way. And I told you that, but you haven't listened, because you don't have any fucking brains. You're too fucking stubborn, saying, No, you can't tell me what to do with my life. You should've listened and you'd've been a lot better off at this point. But you're too fucking stupid. So now you're suffering for it. . . . Amy's young, that's why I took her. Isn't it sick? It took seven days for her to completely forget about you. Isn't that sad? She was tough the first three, but now, the last six have been nothing. It's like, no memory. Totally gone. She doesn't miss you. She doesn't miss Erin, she doesn't know who that is. She doesn't miss anything. Everything is out of her life. Right now she only knows me, and that's who she loves. Daddy. She's in the bathroom here, playin' around. Amy! Come here. Somebody wants to talk to you on the phone. Hahahaha. You want to talk to somebody? Who do you want to talk to? Nope, she's off again. . . . You love her, don't you, Kerry? You miss her? She's your buddy, isn't she? She's got a great face, a great smile. God, she's a beautiful child. She's sitting here, rambling on, ranting and rav— she's a total pain in the ass! Boy, believe me, I tell you, she is tough. She never stops. She eats like a pig. She's eating me out of house and home. I'm broke. She's taking me to the poorhouse. Do you feed your daughter eggs, by the way? Sometimes? Oh, that's kind of you. I know you don't eat 'em, and Erin doesn't get 'em, because of you. Amy, she's had eggs every single day she's been with me. Take care of your kids! Don't style them after you. Amy looks like a ragamuffin. She looks like white trash—Hey, monkey! Come here! You want to sing a song? Or you want to pick your nose. All right, let's go. One, two, three. Jingle bells, jingle bells, jingle all the way. Oh what fun it is to ride in a one-horse open sleigh, hey!—It hurts, doesn't it, Kerry? To hear her. Well, it's lousy, but that's life. Life is cruel. I could not get what I wanted from you, and now the ball's in my court. I have you over a barrel. I don't have to let you talk to her, I don't have to let you see her again. I know you want her. I know. You'll do anything to get her back. Even lie. Well, I'm telling you right now, you're going to get her back. And I'm going to give you a freedom to do whatever you want. But if I find anything out, really, there may not be another chance. Until Vinnie's out of the picture, it's not going to be any different. I just can't live with it. It's never going to be over unless I get my way. So if I give you back the kid, and then two weeks later I'm crazed because I feel that you, you, you wronged me, it'll happen again. There's going to be trouble. It's not going to be nice. I'm going to sit down next to you in a coffee shop somewhere, and you're going to be shocked. And it's going to be the end. Or maybe I'll come and get Erin, too, and they'll both be out of your life. You know I'm very capable of doing stuff like this. Very capable. I was gonna leave the state, and you'd never, never find me. Never. I was on my way out. Gone. History . . . What's all that clicking? You're recording this? You're recording the conversation! So you can have me put away, because I'm a lunatic? But it's not that simple. There was a good article in the paper a while back about the return of the big green death machine. The gas chamber. All the killers on Death Row. Read the article! It shows you what people do. People do crazy things, they're just so riled up and fired up, they don't care what happens to them. They get, they get insane. Do you understand what I've been trying to tell you? I want you to realize that I'm serious, that this is serious. I told you all along I can't live with it. I'm not playing games anymore. This is not a game.

I LISTENED TO the whole thing while standing, as if intending to flee. It felt like a lifetime. And here's what struck me: Gil's jokiness, his madness, the way he turned on a dime; Amy in the background, a toddler singing, sounding happy; and me, whining and sobbing and pleading and lying. *I just want my baby. Give me my baby back. I told you, I'll never see Vinnie again. I'll never talk to him again. I don't care about him. You want me to write it in blood? I'll write it in blood. Please, you have to believe me. Please, please. Just give her back to me. Please.* Then there was Gil's dismissal of Erin, because she'd foiled his plans—how I hated his shrugging *That's life, that's okay.* In forty-five minutes I heard not a single *I love you* or *I loved you*, not one word of tenderness, and no mourning for the loss of my love, only a burn-it-all-down determination to win. But in my voice, too, I heard the desire to win. A spark of defiance I recognize now as life-saving, even if it was wrapped in fear.

IN 1998 *SALON* magazine published an article by Peter Kurth titled "Kidnapped," in which he recounted how his sister Barbara's ex-husband, Stephen H. Fagan, had taken their two young daughters for a weekend visitation in 1979, then disappeared with them for twenty years.

When I first read this story, recognition knocked me sideways.

In the immediate aftermath of her girls' abduction, Barbara Kurth rallied, determined to find them and positive they'd be returned. But as months passed without word, she feared her daughters had truly vanished. Local law enforcement viewed the disappearance as a domestic matter, fallout from the Fagans' vicious divorce, and were reluctant to get involved. Kurth pleaded with state and federal authorities for help; they told her, incorrectly, that the law in Massachusetts did not prohibit parental kidnapping. She tried to get the media's attention, but they ignored her. She ran ads in local newspapers, to no avail. She had Stephen Fagan's uncooperative parents deposed. She even contacted her US senator, who declined to intervene. Years went by. Gradually, Barbara pulled her life together, earning a PhD in biology and remarrying. But she never forgot her daughters; she spent all her savings on private investigators. The girls were located in 1997 only because a relative of Fagan's knew where he was and felt guilty after seeing an episode about the abduction on *America's Most Wanted*. Fagan was arrested at his mansion in Palm Beach, Florida, charged with kidnapping, and extradited to Massachusetts.

During this uncertain period, Barbara kept her distance from her daughters, now twenty-one and twenty-three, partly to avoid legal conflicts but also because she feared they might refuse to speak to her. After so many years of longing for them, she was terrified of rejection. She did write several heartfelt letters, which they ignored.

And then, on the eve of trial, Fagan pleaded guilty. In return he received a suspended three-to-five-year prison sentence, five years of probation, and two thousand hours of community service with a Veterans Administration hospital in Palm Beach. He was also required to make a $100,000 donation in his ex-wife's name to a charity for orphans and troubled kids, which he could easily afford. Barbara's champions were outraged—that was *it*? For stealing a woman's children?

The two young victims supported their father. At a news conference after the pleading, they thanked Fagan for the "many sacrifices made on our behalf" and retroactively gave consent for the actions he'd taken all those years ago.

Erin and Amy, I've always known, would do the same for me.

Yet the more I learned about Stephen Fagan, the more he resembled Gil.

According to Barbara's family, Fagan was a liar and a domineering husband—they called him "the thug." He demanded Barbara say "I love you" at the end of multiple daily phone calls. He made her stand in the front window each morning and wave until he drove out of sight. During the marriage he may have earned most of his money selling stolen art. In divorce papers, Barbara alleged he'd forged checks and stolen identification.

To establish his alternate life in Florida, Fagan had assumed the name of a dead six-year-old boy, William S. Martin, using that child's birth certificate to obtain a driver's license, the classic recommendation of books on how to change your identity. But Fagan added a brazen twist. He became *Doctor* Martin, despite never having attended medical school or earned a PhD. "Bill Martin" told his new socialite friends in Palm Beach he'd worked for the CIA. He said he'd been a foreign advisor to presidents Nixon and Carter. He told everyone, including his two daughters, that the girls' mother had died in a car crash.

Dr. Martin had charm and twice married wealthy women, eliminating the need of a job. He spent his days driving around town in a red Ferrari and hanging out at Donald Trump's country club, Mar-a-Lago. After his arrest, his younger daughter's swim coach at the University of Southern California spoke to a reporter, describing an incident where Dr. Martin had bought coffee and muffins for dozens of people during a power outage. Martin, the coach maintained, was "a very nice guy, a very generous guy—he's very sociable and supportive."

Gil had so often been described in just that way.

I've seen video of Stephen Fagan standing on the courthouse steps after his guilty plea, earnestly insisting he'd done what he had to do. He'd feared for his daughters' lives, as I had feared for Amy and Erin.

Was he my mirror image?

I made myself a chart.

STEPHEN FAGAN/ DR. WILLIAM MARTIN	KERRY/KAREN
• two daughters, 2 and 5 when abducted	• two daughters, 3 and 7 when abducted
• custody pending	• custody awarded, subject to appeal
• illegally assumed false identity	• illegally assumed false identity
• gave children new first and last names	• gave children new last names
• relocated children	• relocated children
• remarried	• remarried
• claimed spouse was abusive and an addict	• claimed spouse was abusive and an addict
• children told other parent was dead	• children know other parent is alive
• daughters loyal to dad, rejecting mom	• daughters loyal to mom, rejecting dad

The comparison was not reassuring.

Only after listening to the recorded phone call with Gil did I see the flaw in this reasoning. Gil had promised murder, whereas

Barbara Kurth wasn't violent. She'd never threatened to kill her husband. She did not own a gun.

Had she been, as Fagan claimed, a drug addict? Had she, as he testified in divorce proceedings, let her daughters run around naked and hungry? Did Fagan save his children's lives by abducting them, or was their disappearance fueled by animus and revenge? Barbara Kurth had had the gall to initiate a divorce—did Fagan see himself as justice's sword, or were his actions an intimate punishment intended to endure through his ex-wife's lifetime?

Without proof, how could anyone know?

Fagan, it seems, had utter faith in his story. He'd cast himself from the get-go as a tragic widower, his daughters' lifeline, their only parent. He never second-guessed his actions and he never looked back. Their first year in Florida, he and the girls lived rent-free with a friend, despite his having fled with enough cash to start a new life. Well, he was a man, with his gender's intrinsic authority. That must have made it easier for others to believe him. He talked his way into an easy life, breezing around in that sportscar, pretending to be a doctor and secure in his alternate identity. Had he expected people to swallow his lies? Did he think, *Look at you all, drinking my Kool-Aid*?

I, on the other hand, never counted on anyone's belief. Hardest of all has been believing myself. Writing this story has been a kind of exorcism, a way of getting rid of the devil in my head who says, even now, that we did not need to run, who insists that depriving a man of his children was, and is, unforgiveable.

A FEW YEARS AGO, I chanced upon something called the Danger Assessment Tool. Developed in the late 1980s by Johns Hopkins University School of Nursing associate dean Jacqueline Campbell, Danger Assessment was based on years of investigation into domestic violence and how certain behaviors, patterns, and social demographics raise or lower a victim's risk of fatality. There are two parts to it. In the first, a calendar tracks individual incidents of violence over the course of a year. Women, as I know well, often doubt their perceptions, and because they tend to underestimate their peril, they remain in the relationship. Some stay because they have young children; some are stymied by medical concerns or a crippling lack of funds. Others continue to love the man who threatens them. The calendar reveals, in black and white, the frequency and severity of abuse.

The second part of Danger Assessment is a yes-or-no questionnaire designed to evaluate immediate jeopardy. The quiz is weighted: answer "yes" to between 18 and 20 questions and the risk of murder is "extreme"; between 14 and 17, risk is "severe"; between 8 and 13, risk is "increased." Some questions are associated with a greater likelihood of fatality: choking; forced sex; being threatened with a weapon; jealousy. The average score for women who are killed is just under 8.

The Danger Assessment Tool is used all over the world, by law enforcement and courts, shelters, advocates, social workers, and healthcare professionals. It is an indispensable diagnostic, because courts still give a man's word more weight, law enforcement still downplays women's fears, and women who are murdered still die most often at the hand of an intimate partner.

Here, for anyone in need of it, is the questionnaire.

1. Has the physical violence increased in severity or frequency over the past year?
2. Does he own a gun?
3. Have you left him after living together during the past year?

4. Is he unemployed?

5. Has he ever used a weapon against you or threatened you with a lethal weapon? (If yes, was the weapon a gun?)

6. Does he threaten to kill you?

7. Has he avoided being arrested for domestic violence?

8. Do you have a child that is not his?

9. Has he ever forced you to have sex when you did not wish to do so?

10. Does he ever try to choke/strangle you or cut off your breathing? (If yes, has he done it more than once, or did it make you pass out or black out or make you dizzy?)

11. Does he use illegal drugs? By drugs, I mean "uppers" or amphetamines, "meth," speed, angel dust, cocaine, "crack," street drugs or mixtures.

12. Is he an alcoholic or problem drinker?

13. Does he control most or all of your daily activities? For instance, does he tell you who you can be friends with, when you can see your family, how much money you can use, or when you can take the car? (If he tries, but you do not let him, check here.)

14. Is he violently and constantly jealous of you? (For instance, does he say: "If I can't have you, no one can?")

15. Have you ever been beaten by him while you were pregnant?

16. Has he ever threatened or tried to commit suicide?

17. Does he threaten to harm your children?

18. Do you believe he is capable of killing you?

19. Does he follow or spy on you, leave threatening notes or messages, destroy your property, or call when you don't want him to?

20. Have you ever threatened or tried to commit suicide?

Of the twenty questions in Danger Assessment, I answered yes to seventeen.

If I'd taken this quiz while married to Gil, I might have gotten out years earlier. Or maybe not. Packing your bags can feel impossible when you're in the thick of a relationship and the damage is all around you. If you do find your way out, the task of leaving mentally remains. That can feel impossible, too. You need someone you trust who will help you *see*. For me, that was Vinnie.

IN 1989, AFTER Gil returned Amy, by the time we got back to the apartment in Santa Cruz, there were already messages on the answering machine. Vinnie and Amy and I fled south the next morning, taking almost nothing. By the time we arrived in Los Angeles, Gil had left a series of increasingly threatening messages on Vinnie's machine. We collected Erin in Carlsbad and said goodbye to Mom. That was so hard; we couldn't stay, we had to go, and everyone cried. Back in LA, we moved briefly into a motel. We closed out our savings. We married. The next day we sold our cars and bought a used Subaru wagon for cash. Then we ran.

It was not without cost.

Once I was Kerry, who struggled to become Karen, who needed an identity credible enough to survive. How ironic it is that only in becoming someone else could I be who I am.

Who would I have been if we hadn't run?

The sense that we remain the same person over time is an illusion, grounded moment by moment in the senses and bound, whether loosely or tightly, to memory. Our thoughts and feelings and sensations are constantly changing, altering who we might be. For each of us there are also shadow selves, the lives we might have lived if things had gone another way. These shadows may be long, and ever-lengthening, so far from what we know of ourselves that they become scarier than anything. They may be invisible, as if it were perpetually high noon.

There is a life in which I was never put up for adoption. Another life where a different family took me. Another where Mom was light-hearted, and Daddy didn't destroy himself with his drinking. Another where I kept my son. Another where, instead of hitchhiking home from the beach at fifteen, I took the damn bus and thus avoided my teenage pregnancy, which led me directly to Gil. There is a life in which Gil never gave Amy back, where I am left bitter and forever grieving. Another where she surfaced after many years and then, like Barbara Kurth's daughters, rejected me. Another where I didn't have an affair and Gil and I stayed married, but our days were filled with misery, or worse. Another where we loved each other and kept our family intact, and he beat his addictions and reformed his criminality.

The what-ifs are dizzying.

How do you know who you are?

Here is what I've come to believe: You are what you do, and what you fail to do, who you love and how you show it. The decisions we make, and the actions we take, follow us through all time. I never doubted Gil's love for the girls, but words are easy. I can only judge by what he did. And me? This is the only definition of identity that's given me peace. Disappearing protected my daughters, and Vinnie, and me. It gave me my life. Mother, daughter, wife; coward, hero, criminal. I did what I had to do. I would do it again.

I am the monster at the end of this book.

I am also the storyteller, with an obligation to truth. The question is: whose truth? Context is all and memory is slippery. In this story Gil becomes who I say he is: a gem, a piece of shit; a good man, a bad man; a man who claimed he'd do anything for his children, and a man I'd never allow around my kids.

Why didn't he look for his daughters? Why didn't he fight for them? I'll never understand it. But sometimes I think he just . . . let us go. Maybe that was a kind of love, shown in the only way available to him.

He is still with me, of course. Rummaging around in my psyche, telling his stories.

Here is one:

A little boy who lives at Eighty-second Street and York Avenue in New York heads off to his first day of school at PS 158. He walks with his older brother through their largely German immigrant neighborhood, but it is not long after the end of World War II and memories are fresh, and there is still an undercurrent of anti-German feeling. The older brother has told the little boy stories about rocks and rotten fruit thrown, and about playground bullying, and the boy is worried. What no one has made clear is that at school everyone speaks only English. The boy, who knows little of that language, spends the hours before his first recess confused and terrified. When the bell rings, instead of going outside to play, he ties his shoelaces to the legs of his desk. He knots them and pulls them tight. When the teacher notices and approaches, he cries. When she tries to undo the laces, he screams. He will be stuck here forever, he thinks, *trapped*, forgetting that he's the one who did the trapping. Finally, someone fetches the older brother off the playground and he comes to free him. He comes to free Gil.

AS I WRITE these words in 2024 Vinnie and I still make our home in LA. But who knows? We are nearing retirement, and changes are coming. Marrying this man remains the best decision I ever made. We began as friends, became lovers, spouses, fugitives, and co-conspirators. Together we raised two strong, loving women who know who they are and fight for a better world.

After ten years in the Navy, with postings all over the map, Amy went civilian. She brought back from her last deployment small chunks of lapis lazuli for Vinnie and me. His looks like the Rock of Gibraltar, mine like the iceberg that sank the Titanic. This strikes us as funny. Amy now makes her home in Portland, Oregon, and works at an architectural engineering firm. Erin met her husband, Eric, when they both clerked for senior federal judges in Washington, DC. In 2010 they married on New Year's Day at the Jefferson Memorial, my daughter in a lace cocktail dress that once belonged to my mom. Now we are grandparents to Adrián, Mateo, and Javi. Erin's boys. I held each when he was newborn, a baby in my arms bringing on storms of emotion, memories of my beloved little girls, and my mother, and my birth mother, and, always and forever, my son. Sometimes the past feels like a face in a window seen, again and again, from a speeding train, and there are no endings, only beginnings.

[ACKNOWLEDGMENTS]

A note about domestic violence: For anyone interested in the subject, Rachel Louise Snyder's *No Visible Bruises* is both an invaluable examination of a seemingly intractable problem and a look at possible solutions. Jess Hill's *See What You Made Me Do* challenges preconceived ideas about domestic violence, shedding light on the insidious nature of abuse. Ginny NiCarthy's *Getting Free* offers victims useful exercises on how to recognize danger, accessible information on current research, and practical advice on things like the pros and cons of entering a shelter. The National Coalition Against Domestic Violence (https://ncadv.org/) is dedicated to supporting survivors and holding offenders accountable. The Battered Women's Justice Project (https://bwjp.org/) promotes systemic change within the civil and criminal justice systems. If you (or a loved one) are suffering now, or feel you are in danger, please call the National Domestic Violence Hotline at 800-799-7233 or text BEGIN or START to 88788. They will move mountains to help.

Parental kidnapping has long been a subject of novels and films, but there are surprisingly few books on the topic; most are self-published personal accounts no less anguishing for their relative obscurity. Maureen Dabbagh's *Parental Kidnapping in America: An Historical and Cultural Analysis* examines how social, political, legal, and religious culture can exacerbate family conflicts and lead to abduction. *The High-Conflict Custody Battle: Protect Yourself and Your*

Kids from a Toxic Divorce, False Accusations, and Parental Alienation, by Amy J. L. Baker, J. Michael Bone, and Brian Ludmer, offers practical advice on navigating the minefield of a difficult divorce. WomensLaw.org provides state-by-state information on available legal remedies.

I READ A lot of material while writing this memoir, much of it unrelated to my story. But casting a wide net is one of the rewards of working on a book—if only we could use everything we learn. For the parts of *She's Under Here* that incorporate outside reporting, I consulted the following works:

First published in 1973, Vincent Bugliosi's *Helter Skelter* remains the definitive account of the 1969 Manson murders in Los Angeles. Several subsequently published books have shed additional light on events. The most helpful to me was Jeff Guinn's *Manson: The Life and Times of Charles Manson*, an absorbing biography that chillingly depicts Manson's world, while also defanging his alleged "mystical powers."

Three book-length investigations into the John List murders differ in minor ways on crucial details, but Joe Sharkey's *Death Sentence: The Inside Story of the John List Murders*, Timothy Benford's *Righteous Carnage: The List Murders in Westfield*, and Austin Goodrich's *Collateral Damage: The John List Story* all gave me a narrative timeline, along with useful psychological portraits of List.

The Beast in the Garden, by David Baron, is an engaging and informative account of the "cougar problem" in Boulder between 1988 and 1991. It also examines the ecology of wild spaces, and especially, the inevitable clash of civilization and nature in suburban landscapes.

As far as I can tell, there have been no books written about Terry

Barton and the Hayman Fire, though a formal report, *Hayman Fire Case Study* (Russell T. Graham, technical editor) was published by the United States Department of Agriculture in 1993 and can be found online, as can numerous newspaper articles about the fire. Most useful for my purposes were online transcriptions of court proceedings from the civil suit brought by several insurance agencies against the Forest Service. Further afield, Laura Mullen's prose poem "Torch Song (Prose Is a Prose Is a Prose)," published in *The Iowa Review* in 2004, shifted my perception of the tragedy, and allowed for a more kaleidoscopic reading.

Peter Kurth's original article in *Salon* about the kidnapping of his sister Barbara's two daughters, and an ABC News transcription of his April 4, 1998, interview on *Good Morning America*, were invaluable aids to understanding the scope of Barbara Kurth's ordeal. Because she and Stephen Fagan had lived and divorced in Massachusetts, the *Boston Globe* was the best source for contemporaneous reporting. Debra Rosenberg's May 1998 *Newsweek* article titled "The Man Who Loved Control" informed my take on Fagan's motivations.

NO STORY EXISTS in a vacuum, and I am forever grateful to Susan Ramer, for her smart agenting, but more importantly, for years of friendship. To Kathy Pories, whose thoughtful edits improved this book immeasurably. To Gregg Kulick for his elegantly mysterious jacket design, and Steve Godwin for an interior design that is both lovely and eminently readable. To Sally Kim, Nadxieli Nieto, Kara Brammer, Marisol Salaman, Brunson Hoole, copyeditor Chris Stamey (who saved my bacon), and to everyone else at Algonquin Books—the house is a gift to readers and writers alike. To the MacDowell Colony, Yaddo, and the Virginia Creative Center for the Arts, for creative support. To my colleagues and soulmates at Lighthouse Writers Workshop: Andrea Dupree, Michael Henry, Erika Krouse, Jennifer Itell, Tiffany Q. Tyson, Juan J. Morales, Suzi Q. Smith, Annie Krabbenschmidt, J. Diego Frey, Roger Wehling, and the late Chris Ransick. To Bethanne Patrick, for years of delightful, writerly conversation. To Jeanne Heifetz, for her connection to the past and loving faith in the future. To Allison Wright, for pulling my essay out of the slush, and to Leslie Jamison, for selecting it for *Best American Essays*; fate works in mysterious ways. And to Richard Nash, the best creative coach in the world. Without him, I never would have finished this book.

Finally, to my family: Elena and John Bourke, Eric Atilano, and Adrián, Mateo, and Javier Palmer Atilano. To Vinnie's late parents, Anna and Vincent; and mine, Dorothy and Ray. And always and forever to Amy, Erin, and Vinnie. I have been lucky in love.